Beautiful Woman

"... risen, empowered, and beautiful to the core."

By Judith Lenore

www.xulonpress.com

Dedication

*B*eautiful Woman is dedicated to my sisters-together-in-Christ (STIC). It was you who told me that I must write this book. You have believed in me, prayed for me, and have learned from me. You have blessed my life and my growth in the Lord.

This is my gift of love and thanks to all of you.

Judith

Acknowledgements

I am not only grateful but also indebted to the Hillsong Women's Colour Your World Conferences in Sydney, Australia. It was the modeling of your leadership and your message that changed my self-perception and consequently my life. Thank you for your passion and devotion that inspires and creates beauty beyond measure.

Thank you to my husband, my children, and my dearest friends and family for praying for me and for this book.

Letter to the Reader

You are of infinite value and worth.
You are a magnificent representation
of the very image of God.
You are truly beautiful!

May 2024
NB

You, dear reader, are a masterpiece of God's infinite love (Psalm 139:4-6 NKJ). He created you out of His love and desire and He wants you to live in that love and desire which knows no limit or defeat. There is absolutely nothing that can ever separate you from His loving and desiring you, forever (Rom. 8:38-39 NIV). Amazing.

My fervent hope and prayer is that by reading this book your eyes will be opened to see yourself differently from the way you have perceived yourself, and from the way others have perceived you. You will embrace an entirely new image of yourself. Beauty will be released in you beyond measure.

You will never be the same again! Amen!

Introduction

Do you know that you have been created as God's magnificent masterpiece? He has created you by divine design with divine purpose. You are chosen, cherished, deeply and intimately loved and blessed beyond measure.

Do you know that you have been given a unique personality with talents, abilities, and gifting? In the entire world there is no one exactly like you. No one else has your smile, your eyes, nose, hands, or voice. Your handwriting is unique and so are you. You have been created as an original, bearing the image of an awesome creative and powerful God.

An image is a representation of the *essence* of an object. You are that *essence* of God. How amazing is that? Discovering your authentic self, your true worth, and your beauty as a woman is a priceless gift that you cannot earn or buy. It is a free gift from God the Creator. All you need to do is search for the Giver with all of your heart and you will not only find the Giver but also the true gift of yourself - the woman you always wanted to be- the woman that seemed just an illusion for you, but who appeared to be real for others.

Yes, you will be surprised, and relieved, as you discover that you are:

the "risen, empowered, and beautiful to the core" daughter of the King!

Welcome to a new you!

Thankyou jesus!
Martha.

Table of Contents

Section I: Discover

Section II: Remember

Section I

Discover

Chapter 1

Searching for Identity:
Affirmation and Approval

I'm sure you have asked yourself the question, "Who am I?" "Who am I deep down on the inside? Do I like the person I see in the mirror?"

Have you at different times in your life entertained the thought of, "What's wrong with me? How come other girls have it easier or better than me? Why don't I measure up to them? Where do I fit in and belong?" We all want to know who we really are and what our life is all about. We all want to be loved, accepted, and to belong; to know that we have deep intrinsic value.

I was very extroverted but empty on the inside, searching for meaning and personal value. I needed to know that I was wanted more than anything else. I didn't have that acceptance and approval for myself deep down on the inside, so I was desperate to receive it on the outside from any and all others.

I needed to accept and love myself
the way God accepts and loves me.

How could I do this when I had
no true picture of God or of myself?

As far back as I can remember I was always confused and mixed up about so many things in life. I lacked peace and confidence in myself because I was very insecure on the inside. I wanted love and attention, and to know that I was valuable and cherished; that I was really wanted. As a young girl I didn't know why some people said bad things about me to my Mom and I didn't know why she never explained those things to me. She just kept working harder at making me appear acceptable.

I had no idea I was God's dearly beloved daughter; a daughter who was loved unconditionally and highly prized by a Heavenly Father. It would have been hard for me to imagine that at the time since I didn't experience being unconditionally loved and cherished by my own earthly father.

Being the result of an unwanted pregnancy was not the best start in life in finding worth and value. Little did I know or understand that a spirit of self- rejection was operative in my life. I always had difficulty in feeling wanted, so guess what I did? I tried really hard to be a "good" girl by pleasing everyone all of the time, and by making sure I was performing well at whatever I did. "Then I will feel wanted and accepted," I said to myself. Does that sound familiar to you? However good it may seem, pleasing people and performing well do not get the results you want. Our intrinsic value doesn't come from the outside.

While growing up I performed in ballet and dance lessons, baton lessons, skating lessons and piano lessons. I performed at school in extra-curricular activities and in the community club baseball teams. I was very busy performing in all these activities and lessons.

Performance and perfectionism
must be the answer.

This is the way to affirmation and approval.

However, whenever I made a mistake, whether at school, on the baseball field, or particularly while playing the piano, my Dad would yell at me and say, " Can't you ever do any-thing right?"

Whenever I failed at performance or perfection it felt like I was a failure.

This wrong conclusion of being a failure (a lie) became a heart belief that produced fear and insecurity.

Believing lies will always produce fear and insecurity within oneself.

Discouragement and disappointment with myself remained hidden in me for many years. "I can't do anything right. I'll make a mistake. I will fail."

I buried my hurt feelings and tried harder to get it right; to make no mistakes or fail at anything. Not getting it right can link your feelings and thoughts to *you* not being right –perceiving yourself as unacceptable because you failed. "There's something wrong with me. What's wrong with me?" That question plagued me from my childhood into adulthood.

Growing up in my particular family structure also created confusion and insecurity for me as a female. My mother was the acting head of our family, as was her mother. My grandmother and grandfather lived downstairs in the three storey house where I lived for the first eight years of my life. I knew my Mom's parents for such a little while because they both died

18

within a week of each other in their early sixties. However, even at a young age I realized that my grandmother was the dominant force in the home, and my grandfather seemed to be quite alright with that.

I didn't see any male servant leadership within our household of three families living together in that small three storey house. As much as I can recall, mostly the women took charge of the household in a position of strength in fulfilling their household and maternal responsibilities, while the men were usually absent or in a position of weakness as victims of alcohol abuse or perpetrators of emotional and sometimes violent outbursts. My grandfather was the only stable and quiet man in the house but he was only in my life for a few short years.

My mom would take care of me and my sisters, attending all the parent-teacher functions, and my Dad would be working on the railroad and drinking at the local bar. Upon returning home he would crawl up the stairs to our tiny third floor bedroom with my Mom waiting at the top of the stairs with questions. I don't remember what happened after that. I remember that one time my grandmother helped him up the stairs and scolded my mom for not caring for him when he was drunk.

Later in life my father became angry and frustrated, unfaithful, and "wandering". He would often criticize, demean, and yell at me; especially about not doing something right or not finishing anything I started. I can't remember him showing up for any of the important events in my life throughout my childhood or adolescence except for a piano recital when I was eleven years old. At that time he was sitting in the audience with my mom but **I had already left the building**. I left the piano recital because of an intense fear of playing in public, and especially in front of my Dad who had constantly criticized me for making a mistake while practicing. I was on my way back home by bus! I was so fearful of making a mistake that I couldn't go out on that stage. The only solution was to run away out of panic. Could that have been my first panic attack???

It's incredibly amazing to me that after I became born-again in Christ I was able to play the piano with ease by ear not only by the written score. I became a Choir Director and Worship Leader never fearing to play in public again. I wrote a mini-musical and taught others how to sing and how to play the piano with love in their hearts. Our God reversed the curse of my fear of making a mistake, particularly on the piano, and He blessed me with confidence and the ability to play from my heart. There is no fear in His love. I am free to make a mistake or to fail (i.e. to not be perfect) without losing my value, self-acceptance or true identity. Apparently no one ever detects if I do miss a note here or there because of the beautiful flow of music on the piano. Amazing.

My father's painful verbal abuse and my crippling fear reinforced the wrong image I had developed of myself as a failure and quitter. My thoughts were filled with the belief that I could not do anything right and that I would not be able to finish what I had started. These had become heart beliefs entrenched in my subconscious. A basic life principle is that you behave as you think. And you think as you believe in your heart (Proverbs 23:7 NKJV).

Emotional abuse produces emotionally hurting people.

Hurting people eventually hurt other people.

I now know that I was not the only female in the house to experience emotional abuse. During my growing up years I always thought I was the only one who had been the object of ridicule and disapproval. So often we think that we are the only one who is experiencing pain, but the Word of God says that anything you or I go through is not unfamiliar to others. We all experience emotional pain and in different ways.

What I didn't know was that my subconscious received these abusive messages as truth, and that created a shame-based personality at my heart level. That shame based unacceptance was buried deep down on the inside of me at an

21

early age and was fuelled by my distorted perceptions and thought patterns throughout adulthood.

Negative experiences of unfair treatment cause negative conclusions about oneself. These negative conclusions based on faulty and distorted perceptions are simply not true.

We feel unloved and unlovable when treated badly by others, subconsciously thinking that we are not worthy of love and respect. **These are Satan's lies.**

All lies are conceived in the nature of Satan who is defined in God's Word as a Liar and Deceiver. He accuses us daily before God (Rev.12:10 NIV). When you are being accused by someone remember that it is Satan behind that accusation. He always wants to deceive you so you will believe a lie about yourself, about others and particularly about God Himself. Thus you enter into the realm of faulty and distorted perceptions and thought patterns. (Reread this until it becomes new revelation to you!)

Anger and frustration accompanied my self-rejection. "Why isn't anyone paying attention to me and loving me the way I want to be loved? "Why can't I do anything right?" In an attempt to relieve the anguish and emptiness I felt deep down, I aimed for perfection in all that I did. I strove for an identity based on human affirmation, and on getting approval based on my performance, perfectionism and popularity. This only fuelled the false image of myself.

My attention was focused on my outward appearance and performance, always aiming to look attractive so that I would attract the attention and affirmation I so desperately needed and desired. Getting good grades pleased my teachers and caused me to feel acceptance and worth so I kept getting good grades- most of the time! Popularity in sports and other extra-curricular activities such as Dance Club and Drama filled my high school years. My teachers and coaches reinforced this type of acceptance and worth.

- I mastered physical appearance and performance to gain acceptance.
- I employed the skill of people–pleasing and pretense in order to belong, and
- I strove for perfection in all that I did to obtain significance.

The world of fashion lured me to the latest fashions (at low cost of course, without designer clothes required) and I was convinced that a new hair color and style was always great for my image. That would make me acceptable and beautiful. . . .I was well on my way to a life of outward "success" and inward defeat.

Looking for attention and acceptance, especially from the opposite sex was almost a preoccupation for me in my attempt to gain affirmation and approval. I think I was as young as eight years old when I had my first "crush" on a boy. I can still remember his name and see that little kiss on my cheek as we played spin the bottle with a group of two girls and four boys. Really, we played spin the bottle! Since I didn't know what it was like to be Daddy's little girl I must have wanted to be anybody's girl!

University life brought more confusion, discouragement, and man hunting! If only I would get asked out by an Engineering student or a Medical student. That would boost my confidence in being wanted and acceptable, especially now that I am a blonde! Yes I colored my hair platinum blonde and I did get asked out several times, but for the wrong reasons. Do all blondes have that trouble? Echoes of my dad's words about women being sex objects lingered in my memory. I guess that's all I'm good for. . .is that my purpose as a woman? Have I been created to be a show piece for a man? Is my purpose as a woman to make a man look good and successful while I lurk in the shadow of anonymity? I found no answers to these silent questions and I found no absolutes. Everything

I learned at university had relativity at its core and ambiguity at its periphery. I wanted truth. . . the absolute truth!

The Feminist Movement had influenced society and the university curriculum to a large extent. I had an underlying "grudge", which was fuelled by what I was learning. I was told that women can make inequality and wrong things right by demanding and protesting. Demand to be equal to a man and to be respected just like a man. Of course I was totally unaware that God had made me equal to man in His sight and placed high regard and honor upon me and all females. Women are not to be treated as inferiors any longer was the strong message I heard from that Feminist era. Equality for all women demanded justice for all women, and that was reason to fight! Although equality, in gender and in the marketplace is a valid right, there was an underlying hostility in their demands. So many women were angry at the authority over them by men in the workplace and in the bedroom!

Why did they want to burn their bras? Such unhappy unfulfilled women with raised fists in the air for justice created more confusion about my true identity and worth. If equal pay for equal work was the only issue addressed with dignity and respect, I think the Feminine Movement at that time (40 years ago) would have made great strides in this area much sooner.

I was so unaware that God had created me equal to a man and that He made me beautiful as man's crowning glory!

I didn't know that there was no real need to long for or demand anything from any man to realize my value and worth.

I hope you are hearing what I am saying. You don't need to demand equality, respect, or acceptance/approval from any man or from anyone else. God has made you acceptable and equal to man not inferior to man. We are different from man not inferior. We have been created as the answer not the problem! Don't quote me as saying women are the answer. This was first stated by Lisa Bevere in Australia at the *Colour Your World Women's World Conference* in 2005.

You have God's approval and acceptance. When He made you He said this is good! Sin is bad, but the creation of your womanhood is good! You are made in His beautiful image, redeemed in Christ, and restored to your feminine heart forever.

As I grew into womanhood, my concept of sexuality was continuing to be formed by how a man viewed me. My efforts were directed at getting a man's attention first and foremost. It was easy and natural for me to play the role of a worldly woman who was out to get a man! I had no idea that my intrinsic value and beauty came from a loving all-powerful God who had created me in His beauty and splendor. I had no idea that my value and beauty were not determined by others' opinions of me, particularly those of a man!

However at that time in my life I needed to attract a man's attention and affection to feel beautiful and acceptable. I tried to be as "attractive" as I could be, according to the world's standards. I knew no other way. If the opposite sex paid attention to me or complimented me, asked me out, or wanted to spend time with me I concluded that I was desirous and beautiful. . .that I was accepted and wanted. Of course that backfired when I was asked out and then expected to "come across" sexually but refused.

I concluded I was not worthy of respect and love, or else I would have been treated differently. I subconsciously believed the lie that I was simply a sex object rather than a person to be known, loved, and cherished. Again the question of, "What's wrong with me?" resurfaced.

The conclusion I made about my female sexuality as a sex object *originated* in the way I was viewed by my father in my teen years. He had wrongly accused me of being promiscuous when I was only 14 years old. His accusatory words were indelibly embedded in my mind. I perceived that I was being objectified or treated as a sex object. This deepened the wrong image I had developed of my sexuality.

Praise the Lord that the emotions and negative conclusions I experienced about myself from such a "view" have been exposed as lies, and now I can *remember those accusatory words without believing them to be true.* There **is** no pain or hatred associated with them any longer. True and lasting forgiveness and healing have erased the wrong perceptions about my sexuality. God's view of my sexuality has redeemed the wrong image I held for all those years. I have not been created as a sex object. I have not been created bad. He has made me good. He has made me beautiful and desirable. He has created me in His image!

Now I think differently. Now I perceive differently.

The truth has set me free!

As I have reflected prayerfully about my Dad, I believe that those accusatory words were the only way my Dad knew to warn me (or scare me) about being promiscuous. He didn't say the right words or have the right tone of love, but I think he wanted to somehow protect me. It was a crude way of doing it, but I now realize that he really knew no other way. Only our God could have opened my eyes to this interpretation and perspective. Amazing!

My Dad had no model for female sexuality other than "sex object" or "mother" figure. And certainly I was not a mother figure to him. It seems very understandable now that he had no other frame of reference for me as a female. I know that God understands each one of us to the depth of our innermost being, including my Dad. My father knew no other way of viewing me. I forgave him with the forgiveness I received from Christ when I became born of the Spirit. Tears stream down my face as I recollect the compassionate unconditional love of God toward all of us.

I no longer have the heart belief that I am a sex object needing to look young and sexy in order to be beautiful, wanted, or powerful! Amazing. Before these lies were exposed I not only carried an underlying disrespect and unacceptance of myself and also disrespect and unacceptance for men in general. **The lie had infected my understanding and perceptions** -somewhat of a Catch-22.

Perceptions determine how we see the world and how we will react to people, demands, issues and circumstances.

Perception is defined as a noun, meaning the ability to see, hear, or become aware of something through the senses.

A highly stressed and hypersensitive disposition usually indicates flawed and faulty perceiving ability due to *preprogrammed distorted perceptions*. That is to say that a person's *internally distorted perceptions have created distortional thought patterns*. Do you remember that my own distorted perceptions and thought patterns were based on lies?

If you perceive wrong you:

- think wrong
- feel wrong and eventually
- do wrong because of those faulty perceptions.

While at Seminary in the Counseling Program I gained several insights that gave me a deeper understanding of wrong identity and false image.

1. Faulty perception originates in observing the habitual coping mechanisms of parents in the family of origin. For example, if your parent(s) would "stuff" their feelings when offended or mistreated and then withdraw to alcohol, prescription drugs or sex, you likely have a predisposition to do the same. *Your perceptions of reality in these circumstances are influenced by their coping habits and you tend to copy the behavior of the adults around you.* You think this is how adults handle the "real world". You have not known or seen anything different.

You consider this to be right. You have determined that your own reality is truth.

2. Most highly stressed individuals are preprogrammed with distorted perceptions to the point that even trivial circumstances or demands can trigger a massive reaction. What do they believe that is not true?

3. When negative thought patterns are broken, painful expectations lose their self-fulfilling power. Irrational, twisted or unrealistic expectations no longer determine how you feel. Rational thinking replaces the negative perception and thought patterns, releasing the person from the corresponding negative feelings. We must not trust our senses to give us an accurate picture of the truth of who we are. Our senses will perceive incorrectly because of deception and lies. Our sensory perceptions must be submitted to God and His Word because God's perspective is the accurate one, His perspective is the truth which sets us free from all falsehood.

I hope and pray that you will identify any wrong conclusions you have drawn about yourself regarding your sexuality. You have not been made as a sex object or the object of a man's domination, but as the *object of God's affection and unconditional love.*

31

Think about the motivation for your physical appearance. Think about the time and money you spend on the outward appearance compared to the time and money spent on your inward self. Think about your family of origin and how the adults viewed each other's sexuality. Ask God to give you His compassionate perspective.

What an impact a father has on a daughter. He is the one to give her the first glimpse of womanhood. Even a baby knows if it is emotionally secure or not. Although both parents need to provide that emotional security, the daughter receives her formative "identity" from the father, just as the son receives his formative identity from the mother. We all need to be re-parented by God our Heavenly Father no matter how bad or how good our family background!

My view of my own sexuality was not redeemed until many years after becoming born again. **No one ever talked to me about the control and influence of my subconscious regarding female identity.** Conclusions about my sexuality were formulated by my earthly father, reinforced by wrong beliefs and then embedded inside my subconscious mind. Our subconscious mind does not filter out thoughts as to good or bad, true or false. It simply grabs hold of them as beliefs.

Whatever you believe with your mind is received and planted as seeds in your subconscious soil.

Later you reap a crop from those seeds because they became heart beliefs.

I'm certain you have heard that what a man sows he will reap. If you believe you are of little value as a daughter and female (sowing), the subconscious will grow a harvest of unacceptance and failure (reaping). I found this to be true for me for a very long time. I hope that writing to you will either prevent or expose wrong beliefs and negative conclusions you may have of yourself. You can reject them with the truths I am presenting to you from God's Word, and disallow the lies in your subconscious to control your self image and identity.

Now back to my living out of the wrong identity and false image. Becoming engaged to someone who I found to be accepting and respectful really escalated my worth and value as a woman. How many young girls are just dreaming to find the right man? How many older women are hoping that the right man will make her life complete? If you're married, you're wanted. This is part of the lie that you need a man to want you in order to be acceptable and loveable. Do not accept the lie as I did!

As long as my fiancé made all the right moves and treated me well I was fine. As soon as he ignored me and gave his attention to another woman I became very angry. Remember how I had been programmed to believe that neglect or rejection, (real or perceived) had created wrong conclusions about myself being unacceptable and unwanted? This always produces fear of lack, and fear of loss.

You cannot be in fear and in faith at the same time.

I was extremely possessive and jealous because I so desperately needed the affirmation and security of knowing I was wanted. What I had actually experienced was the pain of *perceived rejection*. I was angry and hurt because I believed that I was not as important or valued as the other person receiving the time and attention of my fiancé, and that produced hurt covered by anger. "How can I think and feel that way when I was the one engaged?"

Just a note to you about a man's attentions toward a woman. History records that men are drawn by their eye and by their ego, especially to flattery. Don't let this weakness of man determine your own worth! An enticing seductive spirit can lure a man down the wrong path of seduction and victimization. It has nothing to do with your value or acceptance!

The wrong and very confused image I had of myself remained in my subconscious after I received Christ as my personal Savior. Would I ever find the unconditional love, approval, self acceptance, and value I had been looking for all of my life?

Discussion and Application

1. Have you looked to others or to your own personal achievements rather than to God for love and affirmation?
2. What was it like growing up in your home?
3. Describe your relationship with your father and mother and siblings.
4. What or who has influenced your present concept of your self-image most?
5. Define perception. Have you relied upon your own faulty perceptions in assessing your worth?
6. Believing lies produces fear and insecurity. Can you trace any fear or insecurity you may have to a lie you believe?

Chapter 2

The Wrong Identity:
Sin Distorted the True Image

Well it took much longer than I would have expected to discover my true identity and value as a woman. I knew that being a Christian meant that I was a new creation in Christ because my human spirit was born and made alive by connecting me to God. At birth I was born of flesh and blood – a physical birth, and now I am born of the Spirit of God, experiencing a spiritual birth. I have been "born again". Once I had no connection to God because I was dead in my sins and trespasses, and now I am divinely connected to Him through the grace of forgiveness by faith and the power of His Holy Spirit.

However, my soul and body also needed to be
connected to the Life of God in Christ.

I still had all the old thought patterns, based on faulty perceptions, wrong attitudes, and ungodly habits and behaviors.

Even though I knew that God loved me and had forgiven me, I didn't realize that I had been spiritually born into a new Kingdom as a **daughter** of the King. I belonged to royalty as the righteousness of God in Christ through inheritance! I was a co-heir with Jesus Christ, seated with Him at the right Hand of the Father in authority high above all spiritual powers and principalities. **I inherited all this!**

I needed to know the truth about my new identity right down to the core of my being.

Very little emphasis if any was placed on my new spiritual position as a daughter of the King!

I had inherited a new a new identity based on a royal position- a daughter of the King of all kings! I was born into a royal family! How would I discover what that meant?

It was Satan's plan to keep me from discovering my true identity.

Satan's plan was to deceive me into believing that I was still the same old person who would never be completely free of the wrong image and the habitual destructive patterns that held me captive. He had to concede that my spirit was born of God and set free, but he would relentlessly endeavor to keep my soul and body in the bondage of his lies and deception. That false image was still there in my subconscious. My soul had not been made new - yet!

One's identity, or who we think we are can be created by a label that others have put on us, or by conclusions we have drawn about ourselves because of circumstances, background, education, or the way in which others have viewed us. Sometimes we may assume a superiority attitude or either a victim mentality/identity because of the way we have been mistreated. It seems that I had a mixture of these elements creating a wrong identity within my subconscious. Using a dictionary guide, "identity" can be defined as "authentic self"- the real me!

We most definitely need to know the "real me" and *to like* that person. God asks us to love ourselves, just as He loves us. When you love yourself as Christ loves you, you can truly love others. We have failed to realize that we all are born with a false image which makes it impossible to know that real self.

When you don't know or understand yourself, you cannot really know and understand anyone else.

That was the first foundational truth I learned in the Counseling Basics Course at Seminary. That false image becomes a driving force behind behavior, attitude, emotion and reasoning. It is responsible for erecting barriers that prevent the authentic self from being manifest. I had been living my life out of that false image for so many years believing in the wrong identity. Little did I know that Satan, that proud arrogant rebellious angel, had a blueprint for my life that kept me bound to the false image.

He has a blueprint for your life as well. He wants s to keep you captive to the wrong image.

Do you remember the story of an elephant tied to a stake for many years from birth? He was given a radius of 10 feet to roam and to receive food and water. After the stake was completely removed in his adulthood, the elephant continued to roam within that 10 foot radius and no more, in spite of being set free. Mentally and habitually he was still tied to that stake. *It is Satan's plan to keep us believing that we are still tied to a stake! We keep walking within a 10 foot radius!*

Do not let your destructive habitual patterns trick you into believing you have not been set free from their power. That is a lie. *Just because you think or behave in destructive patterns, or function in ungodly habits, it does not mean that their power over you is not broken. The truth must be believed before the thought or action is changed.* The truth according to God Himself declares that Jesus Christ's suffering, death, and resurrection has set you free from the *power* of your sin nature to rule your thoughts, emotions, will, and actions. Jesus has given us a full salvation for spirit, soul, and body.

> *Wholeheartedly believe the truth, reject the lie, and you will be transformed.*

Satan's blueprint for me included a script with a clearly defined role that he and his kingdom of darkness would define. The role I would play was that of an emotionally insecure, fearful, demanding female. Satan would do everything in his deceptive power to keep me from becoming emotionally secure in God's unconditional love, and in the love of the body of Christ. He did not want me to know I was a beloved daughter of the King and highly valued as part of His body. He was completely committed to keeping me from being restored to the image of God, and to preventing me from sharing any testimony of God's goodness in my life.

Girls, Satan hates you and wants to hurt the heart of God by stealing or destroying every-thing that is good in you and in your life. And he will work through people to do it. Never forget this!

He implemented his blueprint for my life during my child-hood, and *the blueprint still remained in my subconscious after I became born of the spirit.* I was still expecting people, partic-ularly those closest to me, to meet all my needs, providing the affirmation and approval I was looking for, while experiencing continual disappointment, anger and deep hurt. I still had the false image of "unwanted" and "bad girl" embedded in my sub-conscious. The truth of the Word of God had not entered that part of me.

Pride feeds an empty mind.
Lust feeds an empty heart.

My heart was empty, craving, and very hungry. Because of deep insecurity, I wanted constant affirmation and undivided attention. However, once affirmed by externals I always felt emptiness within me in a very short time. Satan had produced a stronghold of critical needs that were never satisfied. We all have legitimate needs that God alone will satisfy and Satan knows

41

this, so he simply twists those legitimate needs into demands that are never met.

> *He would do everything to prevent me from having my legitimate needs met, and from discovering the truth in God's Word that declares all my needs are met in and through Jesus Christ.*

God will provide all my needs. Psalm 23:1 clearly states that the Lord is my shepherd and I will not lack anything I need. My focus was not on the truth of the Word of God. Satan focused my attention and actually my heart on what was missing, on what was lacking or what I wasn't and what I didn't have. *Do you notice that Satan still attempts to focus our attention on "lack" or on that which seems out of our reach?*

- Are you focused on lack of what you are not or on what you do not have?
- Are you comparing yourself or your life to others which only robs you of being thankful and faithful to what you already have?
- You have everything you need in Christ! The enemy is a thief who comes to rob, steal and destroy our faith and devotion to a generous Father God Who will supply

all our needs according to His riches in glory in Christ Jesus. Amen!

He is the God of abundance and increase.

Jesus said that". . . I have come that they may have Life and that they may have it more abundantly" (Jn. 10: 10 NKJV).

He has already provided everything you and I will ever need, in Christ. All we need to do is thank Him by faith. And faith works through that awesome unconditional love that is in our hearts by God's Holy Spirit. You and I do not have to earn the right to have all our needs met. We have **inherited** that privilege simply because we belong to Him as His daughters.

Meeting basic human needs for love, acceptance, a sense of belonging, and significance, was an avenue for the devil's devices of deception. He wanted me to have my needs met his way!

Satan's script became even more dramatic. As a new Christian I still confused lust for love. Lust is that human appetite for the many different physical pleasures this world offers. Lust does not only refer to strong sexual desires. Lust is any strong uncontrollable desire for things of the five senses. Remember that I quoted earlier that lust feeds an empty heart that only God can fill. My husband described me as insatiable! And he was right, even though I couldn't see the truth of that outrageous statement at the time. I was not allowing God to meet my need for love and affirmation. I didn't know how. As long as I was in control of meeting my own needs my way there was no submission to God's control.

The old belief patterns of the "fallen" wrong image were still undermining my efforts to live in the spirit of new Life in Christ.

I believed that people, especially my husband and family are supposed to meet my need for unconditional love and affirmation. I was giving love and affirmation to them, believing they are supposed to reciprocate. That's only right and fair I believed. My thoughts and attitudes were part of the old distorted perceptions from my past that were embedded in my subconscious, all based upon this lie of reciprocity. I think there's a colloquialism that says "I'll scratch your back if you scratch mine."

I now realize that this is a struggle we all encounter.

We look to others for the unconditional love and affirmation that only God can supply. Human love runs out. Human love is fickle.

Human love will disappoint and sometimes even destroy us because it is based on selfishness and pride.

But the love of God knows no limits and is never selfish. God's love is the most selfless, unconditional, undemanding, patient, kind, affectionate, ungrudging, humble, enduring, accepting, and non-judgmental divine love to which nothing or no one can compare. Human love will be for you one day and betray you the next day. Sometimes human love will deceive you. All human love is actually rooted in selfishness. It is part of our fallen human nature *apart* from connection with God. Human love is not like God's unconditional love. In 1Corinthians 13 we get a glimpse of the kind of love God has toward us and which He gives to us.

God's [4] Love is patient, love is kind. It does not envy, it does not boast, it is not proud. [5] It does not dishonor others, it is not self-seeking, it is not easily angered, it keeps no record of wrongs. [6] Love does not delight in evil but rejoices with the truth (1Cor. 13:4-6 NIV).

God's Personhood is *never jealous or envious, never boastful or proud, never haughty or selfish or rude. He does not demand His own way. He is not irritable or touchy. He does not hold grudges and will hardly even notice when others do Him wrong. He is never glad about injustice, but rejoices whenever truth wins out. He will be loyal to you no matter what the cost. He will always believe in you, always expect the best of you, and always stand His ground in defending you. That's what our God is like toward each of us!*

As He is, so is Christ. And as Christ is, so are we. Amazing!

Somehow we believe what we experience to be our truth more than the truth of the Word of God. This passage in 1 Corinthians 13 is a description of how God loves us. Our God really is this good toward us and for us! However when we act badly, or sin, Satan brings condemnation upon us, and we think we are "bad" and unlovable, even unforgivable!

Part of the enemy's strategy is that he wants you to believe if you behave badly you deserve to be punished. We forget that the Word of God teaches us the truth! When we behave badly we receive forgiveness as we confess and repent. Our conscience convicts us. It does not condemn us! We are deeply loved, highly valued, and ever blessed. I am still the daughter of the King even though I have made a *mistake, a poor choice, or have sinned intentionally or unknowingly. I am not a bad girl. I am not a bad person. I remain the beloved daughter of the King!*

Our true identity can only be embraced as we uncover and reject the lies that we have believed about ourselves,
about others, and
about our Creator God.

These lies have caused us to perceive incorrectly and to draw wrong conclusions about ourselves. And we have drawn wrong conclusions about others and about God. I have asked for and received God's forgiveness for doing precisely this.

The eye opener is the truth in the Word of God.
Who does God say I am?

- Am I going to believe the false accusations of people who have hurt and mistreated me, misunderstood or judged me? Is this the truth about who I really am?
- Can I confront the image I see in the mirror?

Lies, assumptions, suspicions, doubts and fears were continually fuelling the wrong image I had of myself. The blueprint in my subconscious made me a captive of the darkness because I really believed in the wrong image I had of myself. I had continually yielded to deception and temptation. I was a true born of the Spirit Christian, baptized in water and in the Holy Spirit.

How can this wrong image still control me?

I blamed everyone else including myself for failing to be a victorious Christian. I thought I believed the Word of God. Why was I repeating the same old behaviors over and over? I was completely unaware of Satan's deception and blueprint operating in my life.

- What were the lies I believed about myself?
- What was the fear in my heart?

You can ask yourself the same questions. Approach the Lord's mercy seat of grace and *ask Him to open your heart and mind* to see what you believe that is contrary to His truth and His will for you. As harsh and narrow as it may seem, the Bible teaches us that we belong to God or we belong to the devil. We are either children of Light or children of darkness.

"But you are a chosen people, a royal priesthood, a holy nation, a people belonging to God, that you may declare

the praises of Him who called you out of darkness into His wonderful light" (1 Peter 2:9 NIV).

We either demonstrate the nature of God by walking in the Light (truth) or we demonstrate the nature of Satan by walking in the darkness (deception and lies).

Where do you thoughts originate?

> *You cannot be in the dark and*
> *in the Light at the same time.*

We need a wakeup call to the truth of these Scriptures! If you believe lies you are under the control of the Father of all lies, Satan. What you believe determines how you will think and act. Wrong believing leads to wrong living. Do you see how vital it is to know the truth of who you are in Christ and who God really is?

Before we are born of the Spirit we are all trying to be good, but fail at all our attempts for lasting goodness. When we are born of the Spirit of God we **_are_** good. Not because we have tried harder at being good and have succeeded, but because God has imputed to us His righteousness and goodness through the Lord Jesus Christ. Now we can demonstrate the nature of God. His nature is within us and He will restore us to His very image. Amen! We are good because He said in the Book of

Genesis that everything He created is good (Genesis 1). We have the goodness of God within us. We are good because we have been created in the image of a good God. *It is the sin and the devil that are bad.*

Until I met Christ and this revolutionary truth I had believed that I was bad. Actually I thought that I was part my mom and part my dad! The small good part of me I believed was from my mom and the big bad part of me was from my dad. I knew nothing of the sin nature within myself. I blamed my dad for that. Oops!

> *God has forgiven me and I have for-given my Dad.*
> *I am healed and have relationship with my Dad.*
> *I freely share my faith and love of the Lord with both my Dad and my Mom who each received Christ as personal Savior many years ago.*
> *I am my Dad's primary care-giver as he continues to be medically cared for in a nursing home.*

I came to realize that even though I was born into a new kingdom of Light I still had the wrong image within me.

Sin distorted the true image and Satan devised to keep me bound to sin and to the false image through his deception and lies.

By now you have heard me say this several times. Know the truth and you will not be deceived. The Liar, Deceiver, and Accuser of God's children, roams around like a lion, seeking whom he may devour (1Pet.5:8 NIV).

Satan cannot see into our hearts, but he can see our actions and hear our words.

Please remember this!

Yes he watches to see if we are living in faith or in fear. He can hear our words and see our actions even though *he is not omnipresent or omnipotent.* The Bible lets us know that out of the abundance of the heart the mouth speaks. Therefore Satan has a very good chance of determining our heart condition and using it against us as we speak contrary to the truth of God's Word. It is so crucial that our hearts be purified of sinful thoughts and emotions, and actions.

Our heart attitude establishes things in the spiritual realm.

51

*Then our actions and words establish
them in the natural realm.
This is a process and partnership
with the Holy Spirit.*

Honest confession and forgiveness frees us from remaining in the darkness of sin. We enjoy His love and fellowship once again. We can praise and thank Him and worship Him in spirit and in truth- in word and indeed. His grace for us is without limit. "God resists the proud, but gives grace to the humble" (James 4:6b NKJ). He has made a way to be free of the power of sin forever!

Having a false image and a belief in the wrong identity breeds sin and failure within oneself.

Before I knew my Savior and Lord, I not only carried anger and hatred in my heart against those people who had mistreated and labeled me, but I also had carried unknown anger and hatred toward myself.

Whatever was done and/or said to you that was hurtful or degrading, is capable of depositing sinful thoughts and feelings *in your subconscious about yourself and toward others.* This gives the false image power to remain alive. Without being healed of our wounds, we will carry self-pity, self-righteousness, unforgiveness, bitterness and the possibility of a strong desire for retribution.

Negative conclusions I had believed about myself and about those who had hurt me through betrayal, neglect, emotional or sexual abuse, were exposed. I discovered that these negative and very hurtful thought patterns were rooted in assumptions and beliefs based on lies. And these had been buried deep in my heart. Remember how powerful faulty perception is.

I needed a new relationship not only with God but also with myself; one that would be based on truth!

Do you need a new relationship with yourself?

Satan is described in the Bible as the Father of all lies and the Deceiver! He wants us to spend our time and energy in self-pity for all our ugly stories of unfair treatment and abuse, and he aims at seducing us into believing we need to make all the wrongs right- to bring justice and to bring it our way. That kind of thinking will not bring the deliverance and healing you need to possess your true identity. *We all need to recognize the false negative conclusions we make about ourselves and how we perceive ourselves when treated unfairly, neglected or abused.*

These negative conclusions are based on lies, and all lies come from Satan, who is the real enemy of all God's children. He is your arch enemy. Confess the negative conclusions you have believed about yourself- those that are contrary to what God says about who you are. These conclusions are not the truth. Receive His forgiveness, forgive yourself, and choose to believe God's truth.

Hope you got that!

Discussion and Application

1. What image do you have of yourself? Are your thoughts based on how God sees you and what He says about you? What blueprint are you acting out?
2. Do you have any wrong conclusions about yourself because of labels from your past?
3. What lies have you believed about yourself because of wrong conclusions?
4. Can you think of the people in your life that have hurt you?

    Take a few moments of quiet reflection and ask the Holy Spirit to reveal any unhealed wounds in your life.
5. Do these unhealed wounds cause you to sin when you least expect it?
6. Recognize the pain. Confess to yourself, to God, and to one another and you will be healed.

    The Bible teaches us that as we confess our faults one to another we are healed. As we are honest about any wrong or sinful attitudes or thoughts we may have toward those who have hurt us they can be released and forgiven. *Sometimes we hold our own sin against ourselves!* We need to release our hurts and suffering into the Hand of a loving forgiving God and we can do this before trusted sisters in Christ. Throw away the negative conclusions about yourself.

Receive forgiveness, love, and grace from Jesus for all your sinful reactions to those who have mistreated you.

Forgive yourself!

He understands you completely and sees your heart. There is nothing that has come upon you that has not been present in the lives of other believers, especially common to your sisters in Christ. Satan is not creative. He uses the same devices over and over on all of us.

7. Ask Jesus your Lord to show you why it hurt you so much.

It amazes me to find the answer to that question. Why did I become so angry and upset at the offence? What did I want from that person or persons that I didn't get? Did that person really have the capacity to give what I wanted or needed from them? These are the right questions to ask the Lord.Don't pretend you're ok when you're hurting. Don't bury your anger or run and hide like I did. It will take far too long to get to where God wants to take you.

Release the pain to the Lord and believe you will receive what you want and need from Him, in His way and in His time.

Receive His forgiveness and unconditional love and healing.

Choose to release that same forgiveness toward others.

Grieve the loss, and allow the Living Word and Lord to heal you. His compassions never fail and His love toward you never ceases!

He is faithful!

An Important Note on Grieving

Loss of someone you have loved due to death, divorce, illness, or loss of a job, of a home, of finances, loss of a friendship, loss of a dream etc. all involve sadness, sorrow, and disappointment. Age makes no difference. When we experience any type of loss we need time to grieve that loss. Grieving brings the healing. We all need to grieve but we do not need to be left alone or sink into depression, even though the grieving process creates fatigue and exhaustion. At times of grieving you will feel alone and down. Releasing feelings that identify difficult or negative emotions is part of the process of grieving which leads to healing. Don't deny those emotions.

The Lord is at your side to help you through the grieving process, and trusted sisters-in -Christ will be there for you as well. Do you remember King David's expression of emotion in his deep grief at the death of his son? What did he do next?

We do not grieve as those without hope.

Recognize the 5 Stages of Grieving

1. Denial
2. Anger
3. Bargaining with God
4. Acceptance
5. Relinquishing

Do not hesitate to seek godly counseling at those times of deep uncontrollable grief. I really didn't know how to grieve in a healthy manner for so much of my life. Now I counsel those who need someone to walk through the process with them. Amazing what God can do!

He will heal you and set you free from all the pain and shame you may be carrying in your subconscious.

He will fulfill all your unmet needs and longings.

You will be able by His grace to embrace a new nature with a new identity as the "risen, empowered, and beautiful to the core" daughter of the King!

Yes this is the truth.

Chapter 3

Where did this Wrong Image Originate?

According to the Book of Genesis, at the beginning of Creation, in the beautiful Garden of Eden, God took a rib from Adam's side and fashioned a suitable companion for him in the very image of God. This true image became marred by sin, producing a false image which undermined what God originally intended. Eve was the first woman to be deceived and "fallen." The term "fallen" means separation from intimate connection with God her Creator. When you "fall from His grace" you are not "in fellowship with God".

Sin is defined as anything (thought, action, feeling, or attitude) that *goes against the character or nature of God and His commands and ways;* of not adhering to or yielding to God's divine law. Sin also contains the meaning of *independence* from God rather than dependence upon God, *rebelling against or turning away from what God has ordained,* rather than obeying what God has ordained. *Sin* may be intentional or unintentional.

In Genesis Chapter 3, we hear Eve's conversation with a very attractive and alluring creature, Satan in disguise. He tempted Eve with the lie that if she would eat the forbidden fruit she would be like God, and able to distinguish good from evil (Gen.3:4, 5 NKJ). *Satan led her to think that she was lacking something; that she needed to be more than she was.* Have you ever had this thought about yourself? Can you guess where that thought originated? Eve believed the lie that she needed to be more than she was - that she was lacking something to be fully acceptable - that she needed to become more like God. She failed to realize or perhaps she simply forgot that *she was already like God*! *God created Eve in His image without any lack. She was complete in Him. And God made her heart to desire all that was good.*

All Satan had to do was convince Eve that what he tempted her to do was good.

How many times do you use your own evaluation for what seems good in your own eyes, rather than assessing it by what God says is good?

Eve had no desire to do wrong, so the suggestion seemed right in her eyes. She will become wise just like God. "And it seemed good, to her "(Gen.3:6 NKJ). If only Eve would have remembered that God already made her just like Himself. She was already like God, a representation of God, created in His image. She didn't need to have any more of God. He gave all His godliness to her and to Adam. *He withheld nothing from Adam and Eve except the right to rule over their own lives by their own authority and judgment.* In obeying the suggestion of Satan, she disobeyed God's command not to eat of the Tree of the Knowledge of Good and Evil. Did she forget who she was and all that she possessed? She acted independently.

> *Deception had baited her to sin. This act of disobedience defied God's authority over her life.*

How easy it is to defy God's authority over our lives by simply doing what we think is right or good in our own eyes! (Judges 21:25; Prov. 21:2NKJ). Do not be deceived! When we do this we disregard Jesus as Lord of our life and disobey the commands of God. And it is precisely His Lordship that safeguards us against the attacks and scheming devices of our enemy, Satan. When we think or act as if we are able to handle life on our own, we become our own god and lord, yielding to the temptation of the devil. God does not tempt us (Jas.1:13 ELB).

God told Adam (and Adam told Eve) not to eat from the Tree of the Knowledge of Good and Evil. If they do, they will become their own gods! How vital it is for us to know the commands of God as clearly stated in Scripture. *Know for yourself firsthand. Eve heard the command second hand from Adam, making her more vulnerable to deception.*

*Aim to hear directly from God
in His Word and by His Spirit.
Seek confirmation from counselors of
godly wisdom.*

God the Creator is the Ruler Supreme of all Life and the Judge of the whole earth. All authority to rule and reign belongs to the Creator. Eve was created to reign and to rule with Adam by God's authority and in total dependence upon Him. Eve acted independently from the authority of God and her husband.

The Word of God teaches us to submit to the Lordship of Jesus and then to resist or say no to the temptations of the devil (Jas.4: 7, 8 NIV). Satan and his demons have to leave our presence upon our command *as we come under the Lordship of Jesus*. We need to run to Jesus and speak out loud saying "no "to the temptation, verbally rebuking the devil who is tempting us to sin. We have been given delegated Kingdom authority over our enemy. The temptation comes from the Tempter who deceives and lures us away from the truth by appealing to our natural senses - our flesh. We are not being tempted by God (Jas.1:13 ELB). Remember not to make decisions based upon faulty perceptions. Run to Jesus!

Can you understand more clearly how the enemy of your soul works cunningly to devise appealing temptations to bait you?

Consequences in the Garden

The fatal consequence of sin is death- spiritual death- a disconnection from God. Because the Garden of Eden (of Perfection) was created for sinless humanity, Adam and Eve gave God no other choice but to expel them to a life apart from that Garden and from His eternal life. They would no longer be drawing on eternal life from their Creator. A personal intimate relationship with God had ended. This however did not stop God from continuing to love them even though Adam and Eve and the rest of humanity would attempt life on their own, spiritually separated from their Loving Creator.

Adam and Eve saw each other's nakedness with shame and embarrassment and immediately took fig leaves to cover themselves. Previously Adam and Eve were naked before each other and unashamed. The act of disobedience by Eve and Adam resulted in embarrassment, shame, guilt, and blame, erecting barriers between them and God and a barrier between each other. In fear they hid from God and they would eventually hide from knowing one another, forfeiting intimacy with God and with each other.

In marriage, this usually leads to an inevitable breakdown of physical intimacy as well. In the same way, when we hide in fear from God we shut down the lines of communication and fail to expose our sins and secret thoughts to Him. We hide our true feelings and forget how to be honest and open. We erect a barrier with God and with others. Relationships become strained and fragmented, and personal godliness and fulfillment seem like a fairy tale miles away. This shame, guilt, embarrassment and blame will prevent you from having a healthy and honest relationship with yourself as well. You will hide from others and from yourself.(Confession really is good for the soul!)

Satan uses all these destructive emotions to perpetuate lies and a spirit of fear. You should know that all Satan's lies are rooted in a spirit of fear!

Do you see where all your troubles and sin originate?

Eve lost her true identity and would now live in the fallen false image of sinful humanity.

More Consequences

- As women, this inherited false image will produce a distorted view of womanhood, of relationships, and of direction and purpose.
- Apart from Christ we will become consumed with the world's standard of beauty, acceptance, and significance.
- We will struggle in competition with other women to become beautiful and desirable.
- We will never be contented and completely fulfilled.

How damaging and futile to live in a false image!

This is a long way from loving God,
loving ourselves and
loving others as Christ loves us.

The devil hates us. He hates that we have been created in God's beautiful image; that God loves us and shares His Kingdom with us. He hates our faith and trust in God. He hates God, and desires to separate us from dependency, intimacy, and purpose. He always wants to deceive us. Don't let your natural mind or emotion rule your decision making. That is Satan's domain and he relentlessly wages an internal war against our minds. Joyce Meyer's book and Devotional entitled <u>Battlefield of the Mind</u> is an excellent resource in understanding this battlefield.

Why Does Satan Continue to Tempt us to Sin?

Here are 5 main reasons.

1. Unconfessed sin separates us from God, from self, and from others.

Satan hates for us to have relationship and fellowship with God and with others. He knows the power of unity and joined purpose. His desire is for us to be estranged from God, unknown to ourselves, and isolated from others. He places condemnation upon us so that we will not respond to the conviction of the Holy Spirit but withdraw, remaining in disconnect with God, ourselves, and others.

2. Unconfessed sin leads to sickness and disease: physical, mental, emotional, relational, and spiritual.

Medical science recognizes the effects of guilt, shame, and fear upon the human body; psychosomatic illnesses are traced to problems of the soul, whether emotional or/and psychological. *Addictions, eating/sleeping disorders, high blood pressure, high cholesterol, ulcers, skin rashes, heart attacks/strokes etc. can often be traced back to unknown or unconfessed sin.* Without the forgiveness and continual cleansing from sin, that sin exerts power over us. Sin makes us sick one way or another; secret sin cannot coexist with inner peace. King David illustrated this biblical principle when he attempted to cover his sin of adultery and premeditated murder. In his book Guilt: Where Psychology and Religion Meet it actually records sickness rooted in emotional problems. Dr. David Belgum estimates that 75% of the people hospitalized with physical illnesses have sickness rooted in emotional problems. He concluded that their physical symptoms and breakdowns are, for many, their involuntary confessions of guilt.

Guilt that is unconfessed, unforgiven, or unresolved eventually creates shame, and shame keeps you paralyzed in the past. A person feels guilty because he did something wrong. And that God given guilt should lead to confession and forgiveness. Shame says **you are** wrong, **you** are unacceptable. It makes you hide. Shame is the language of the thief who comes to rob, steal and destroy. Satan keeps us bound by shame.

Grace is the language of Jesus.

Grace sets us free!

Worry alone is a form of mental torture, and it is actually disobedience to the command of scripture to cast all our care (anxiety, worries, concerns, fears)) upon the Lord for He cares about everything that concerns us (1 Peter 5: 6,7NIV). Carrying our worries is actually sin (disobedience and nonconformity to the character and ways of God). It is a form of pride that is saying we can handle these cares and concerns on our own. It is that attitude of independence from God that allowed sin in the Garden!

Unforgiveness, bitterness, envy, jealousy and resentment create relational sickness. Unhealthy relationships can often, if not always be traced back to unknown or un-confessed sin. Our spirit can be sick if we have unconfessed sin toward God or our self. Spiritual conflicts within oneself will eventually produce psychological turmoil, robbing one of experiencing God's peace and love. I have experienced the pain of psychosomatic illness and unhealthy relationships. Praise God He has been my Healer from both! He "forgives all your iniquities and heals all your diseases "(Ps.103:3 NIV).

Finally I confessed all my sins to You and stopped trying to hide them. I said to myself, "I will confess my rebellion to the Lord", and You forgave me! All my guilt is gone" (Ps. 32:5NIV).

We are immediately forgiven when we confess our sins to Him with sincerity and humility. We are cleansed from the guilt and shame of every wrong! (1 John 1: 9ELB). Amazing.

3. Sickness and disease rob us of our full salvation.

What we need to know is that the power of sin *and its consequences* has been broken. Jesus suffered and died not only to pay the penalty for sin and forgive us, but also to break its power over us! Psalm 103 declares that He forgives us *all* our iniquities and heals *all* our diseases. We no longer need to suffer in guilt and shame and all the dreadful consequences of living in the lusts of our flesh.

"Surely He has borne our griefs (sicknesses, weaknesses, and distresses) and carried our sorrows and pains (of punishment), . . . wounded for our transgressions, He

was bruised for our guilt and iniquities; the chastisement (needful to attain) peace and well-being for us was upon Him and with the stripes (that wounded Him) we are healed and made whole" (Isaiah 53:4,5 ELB).

4. We give up and lose faith in God and question His word.

We live like the world instead of demonstrating the ways of the Kingdom. We lose God's perspective. We give in to the lust of the eyes, the lust of the flesh, and the pride of worldly pursuits. *Choosing the ways of the world inevitably causes us to give up on God's Word, which creates more discouragement, double minded-ness, and confusion. The best solution and therapy for this is faith.*

Satan always aims to rob you of your faith and trust in God by tempting you to yield to his deception. He is a Liar, and is known as the Father of lies. Don't believe him! Following the ways of the world does not lead to the faith, hope, and love we need.

5. We have no testimony!

The Book of Revelation clearly informs us that above all else, Satan wants to rob us of our testimony, testifying of God's unconditional unfailing love and goodness, and of the absolute truth of His Word. Satan does not want us or anyone else to believe that God's love is unconditional and forever; that He is for us and good all the time! Satan aims for you to believe that God is holding out on you and that He will not perform and fulfill His Word in your life. He is a Liar!

"The Lord is my Shepherd I shall not want" (Psalm 23:1 NKJ). The New International version translation states that "I shall lack nothing" (PS.23:1). God is divine, everlasting, unconditional love, and God is good, all the time! He always has our best interest in mind and will do whatever it takes to rescue us, to fight for us, to comfort us, to enable us to complete the good work He has begun in us (Phil.1:6 NIV). We shall lack nothing! He is not holding out on you!

Discussion and Application

1. Have you ever thought that you need to be more or do more to be acceptable? Where do those thoughts originate?

2. Define temptation and sin clarifying the difference. Who tempts us to sin? Why?

3. How do you hear directly from God? Why?

4. How has the fallen image distorted your view of womanhood, relationships, direction and purpose?

    Are you living by the truth of scripture or by what you have been experiencing?

5. In Christ you are forgiven and cleansed and made new. Have you received the unconditional love of God and His affirmation for who He has created you to be?

6. Ask God to show you when have you acted upon something that you thought was right in your own eyes, but proved to be wrong according to His standards? What can you see differently now?

7. Until we have knowledge of what God calls "good" we lean on our own knowledge, perceptions and understanding. Have you acted upon something that looked good or seemed right but it wasn't? Can you identify with Eve in being "tricked"/ deceived?

8. **Repentance:** changing our own thoughts and beliefs to agree with God's thoughts and beliefs. We simply confess that we are wrong and agree that He is right! Can you agree with God that He is right all the time? Do you have any area of doubt, misunderstanding, or struggle with believing this?

Agree with God's Word and you will stop
seeing what is missing in your life.
Embrace gratitude for the abundance
that is already present.
Eve had everything she needed
to be all that she desired!

How about you?

Chapter 4

God's Blueprint: The True Image

New Identity

God has a new blueprint for you; one that is based on His unconditional love and truth. Christ has broken the power of Satan's blueprint and wrong image. When Jesus hung on the cross saying "It is finished," He completed His mission of paying the penalty for *all* our sins and sinful nature. We are completely forgiven and free from the distorted image caused by sin and its power. God's blueprint for you is one that is based on His unconditional love and truth!

Where Do You Find God's Blueprint?

Genesis Chapters 1, 2, and 3 give us the account of God's design and purpose for creating woman. He never designed you to be a reproduction of this world. He designed you as a unique and highly valued partner with Himself. *Women do not hold the position of first created but we hold the honor of being the crowning finale!* How awesome is that? We are man's "crowning glory" created as co-heirs with God and man (humankind) of the inheritance given in the Garden. The Hebrew word for "man" in this context is *"adam"* which is translated as humankind.

Woman was designed from the rib of a man to give to "man"(humankind) that which he did not have - a suitable companion and inspiring helper; one who can cultivate relationship and assist in administrating the duties of ruling in the Garden. That is a powerful vision for our lives.

Woman was created by God as the answer to "man's" aloneness.

You are not the problem.
You are created as the answer!

Let's go back to the Garden to see what God's Word says about the masterpiece He has created. Then we will look at Psalm 139 which discloses more of His intimate knowledge of us as His divine creation.

"Then God said, Let us make man in Our image, according to Our likeness: let them have dominion over the fish of the sea, over the birds of the air, and over the cattle, over all

the earth and over every creeping thing that creeps on the earth" (Genesis 1:26 NKJ).

"So God created man in His own image: in the image of God He created him; male and female He created them" (Genesis 1:27 NKJ).

"Then God blessed them, and God said to them, "Be fruitful and multiply; fill the earth and subdue it; have dominion over the fish of the sea, over the birds of the air, and over every living thing that moves on the earth" (Genesis 1:28 NKJ).

Woman was made in the image of God as a *representation* of God not a duplication of God. There is only One God.

She shall represent the qualities of her Creator in His essence, as He has designed her to be.

God has designed us to represent Himself. Any deviation from His essence is a misrepresentation of who He really is. How many times have we misrepresented God as a Christian woman and as the church?

We were never created to be our own god. Currently there is a growing trend toward "designer" gods just as we have our designer clothing. To me this means that we can fashion our idea of God according to what suits our preferences and what makes us look good! Can we say that these designer gods exist to promote our own image rather than representing the image of God in Christ? Jesus never came to make Himself look good. He is good. He is God!

Only the Word of God paints a true picture of who God is.

- Our Father God is the Creator not mother earth.
- Jesus Christ crucified and risen from the dead is our Savior. The good works of mankind cannot justify us or save us from the penalty for our sinful disobedient nature.
- The Holy Spirit, not positive psychology or self-actualization, strengthens and empowers us to live the abundant life.

Genesis 2 describes exactly how the true God created the man and the woman.

"And the Lord God formed man of the dust of the ground, and breathed into his nostrils the breath of life; and man became a living being" (Genesis.2:7 NKJ).

"And the Lord God said, "It is not good that man should be alone; I will make him a helper comparable to him". . . (Gen. 2: 18NKJ).

"And the Lord God caused a deep sleep to fall on Adam, and he slept; and He took one of his ribs and closed up the flesh in its place. Then the rib which the Lord God had taken from man He made into a woman and He brought her to the man.

And Adam said: "This is now bone of my bones and flesh of my flesh;

She shall be called Woman, because she was taken out of Man" (Genesis 2: 21-23 NKJ).

Woman was the only suitable companion for Adam. She was made comparable to man to walk alongside him in union together with God. She was not made lower than man or superior to man. *She was made as his equal, only different from him in design and function.* God made Adam from the dust of the ground; He made Eve from the rib as man's crowning glory.

Both would need each other in representing the collective image of God.

Loving companionship was part of God's intentions for the man and the woman as humans. They belong together as His family. Today, as the family of God, we still belong together. We are the body of Christ "attached" to Christ our Head, and we belong to each other in loving companionship and in mutual care. God's purpose is to make us, His body, one in spirit and in truth as He is one with Jesus and the Holy Spirit.(Gen.29:14 NIV). There is no division or competition in the Godhead. There is no division in the unity of the Spirit and Truth which binds us together with chords of His love. Only the love of God for us and in us collectively can create the desired unity of Spirit and Truth. If you have the Spirit and Truth you will sense His love and companionship with each other.

In a marriage relationship husbands *"ought to love their wives as their own bodies; he who loves his wife loves himself" (Eph.5:28NKJ).* He is the image and glory of God; woman is the glory of man. And you wives must submit to your husbands' leadership in the same way you submit to the Lord. . . for a husband is to care for and love his wife the way Christ cares for and loves the church. *"So you wives must willingly obey your husbands in everything, just as the Church obeys Christ" (Ephesians 5:22-24 NKJ).* For man is not from woman, but woman from man.

Think about that for a minute. Woman is from man; handpicked by God as the answer to man's aloneness. *"Nor was man created for the woman, but the woman for the man. . .for as woman came from man, even so man also comes through woman; but all things are from God" (1 Cor.11:7b; 8; 12NKJ).*

Woman was created to bring God's love and abundant Life where there is no love or life. It shouldn't seem strange that you are placed in families, in marriages, and other situations that call for love and for abundant Life. We are Life-givers and we literally give birth to new life. As women-in-Christ we carry the seed of God's love and Life within us. You certainly do not need to be married to enjoy such fulfillment and joy. All of God's daughters are married first and foremost to the Lord and can share His love and abundant Life with others. Don't let Satan convince you otherwise.

God has made us and anointed us to be Lovers of Christ and Bearers of Truth!

We see that the standard for Christian relationships and for the church is mutual dependence of man upon woman and woman upon man, as they both depend upon God. Whether married or single we are the Bride of Christ, betrothed to Him above all others.

Our intimacy with Him is our place of power.

Our power does not come from our gender! Present feminist movements promote Feminine Power through evolving awareness of "god" within womanhood. It is a secular parallel to the power of biblical sisterhood in Christ. This appears to be an ever-growing movement that draws women into fulfilling their own desires by harnessing some god-like power within themselves apart from salvation and the gift of the Holy Spirit. How alluring this concept presents itself even though it is birthed in deception. It will only lead to a dead end, literally! We need to reach women who are being deceived by such "vain philosophies" with a clear message of the simplicity and power of the gospel. Amen?

Dominion over all the earth is the functional representation of being made in the image of God.

Now that is power! Men and women together are to be God's visible representatives, ruling creation as God would rule it, with loving stewardship. Adam and Eve were given charge over the Garden in order to take care of it. With that power came responsibility to our distinctive dignity under God. God trusted Adam and Eve to be His companions and His co-heirs and co –laborers. They were created not only to have friendship but also to possess authority over all God's creation. He commanded them to be fruitful and multiply! God is a God of increase and productivity. He wanted His family to inherit the earth. All He asked in return was obedience to His will. Adam and Eve had everything any human being could ever want or need.

As daughters of the King we have a mandate from heaven to fulfill God's will here on earth as it is in heaven.

Whatever our status, God's purpose does not change. We are His daughters who are called to know Him, love Him with all our hearts, minds and strength, and to fulfill His *will to "publish" the good news of our value, worth, and our beauty as the created image of God. Amen?*

We make Him known through our redeemed transformed lives, showing others the path of Life. We are lovers and Life-givers endued with the power of the Holy Spirit and the graciousness of God through Christ. God has made this possible by faith and grace through our Savior and Lord Jesus the Christ, the anointed One.

We desire to submit to His leadership because we know His unconditional love and full acceptance. His grace enables us to submit and yield to His Law of Agape love.

- We can submit to His leadership because we experience His unconditional love and acceptance.
- We can submit to His leadership because we know that what He wants is always for our good and His glory.
- We can submit to His leadership because we belong to Him.
- We can believe that His kingdom within us reigns on earth as it is in heaven.

God's desires and purposes always involve what is best for our well-being. He knows us best, loves us more than we can imagine, and believes in us always. We are His treasured possession and great delight. He loves being close to us and longs for intimacy and unbroken fellowship. He has chosen us to reign and rule over the earth with Him.

He has created us to reign and rule over the earth with Him.

He created us out of His love for love – a love that transcends our natural affections and preferences. His agape love goes beyond what we are capable of in our human love and affection. God has chosen to put His super on our natural so we are enabled by His grace to agape love the unlovely.

Do you know that Jesus was described in Isaiah as the ***"root out of dry ground. . . despised and rejected" (Isa. 53:2, 3 ELB),*** and in Him there was nothing attractive physically? How can that be when He was described as altogether lovely?

There is something beautiful in our spirit that transcends our physical appearance and that is the beauty of a gentle and quiet spirit. There is beauty in a life resurrected in forgiveness, grace, and mercy, displayed in His compassions that never fail us. His compassions are new every morning for us and in us! Believe it with all of your heart. Christ lives in you to make you truly beautiful! We can live in His faithfulness, and in His enabling power called grace. Signs and wonders follow us. Those who were lost become part of the family. Those who were blind can see. Those who were lame can walk. Those who were bruised are healed and those who were oppressed are set free. We are clothed in the beauty of humility with the garments of salvation. Such joy!

Especially remarkable is that His love reaches the unlovable, and His mercy reaches the undeserving. Does someone you know need the mercy and love of God through you? While we were still sinning against God and one another Christ came to rescue us with His merciful forgiveness and gracious love. He didn't tell us to shape up before He forgave us and healed us. He never said you or I were too down or too dirty to receive His merciful and gracious love. Can you and I say the same of ourselves toward others?

Do you receive the mercy and gracious love of God for yourself?

When we receive His mercy and grace we have something to give to others. Giving His mercy and love to the least deserving is truly a sign of the resurrected Christ within us. I think it's probably close to being a living sacrifice as commanded in Scripture (Rom.12:1, 2 ELB). Giving love without expecting anything in return is a work of His grace. What magnificent beauty is displayed in such a woman! This is the design and blueprint of God.

God's blueprint is designed to bless and prosper us in every area of our life.

Satan's blueprint is designed to rob, to steal, and to destroy in every area of our life.

As you yield yourself to God's fabulous design, you will find that you are being transformed into godliness with contentment. Yes you will fulfill the role for which you have been created. The role is not that of a selfish demanding insecure female. The image God had in mind for you is one of beauty, strength, and purpose. Your confidence and security come from God's love and approval and you will never need to look for that from others, particularly from men. You are a joint-heir with Jesus, a co-laborer with God and with man, exercising delegated dominion and authority in the earth. Can you believe it?

Proverbs 31 gives us a description of wisdom and personifies wisdom as a woman, attributing to her (wisdom) the qualities that make one successful in personal and public life. The Proverbs 31 woman is not a wimp or a witch! A renowned religious scholar, St. Augustine referred to woman as evil and seducing. Those words do not apply to God's design for a woman. Sin is evil and Satan is a seducer. Unredeemed woman operating in the false image definitely has been influenced by both, but it is the **evil and the sin that is wrong, not the creation of woman. Please never forget that.** Joan of Arc was burned at the stake as a witch because men believed she was evil.

History has shown us many wrong views of women which are not at all what God intended. St. Augustine was wrong. God is right! God did not make you evil or wrong. He made you right according to His image. **It is only sin that made all of us flawed and prone to evil.** Satan has always known this. It's about time we did also. I wish someone would have clarified that for me ages ago. We are beautifully created and will be magnificently restored! It's never too late to be delivered, healed, and set free to rule and reign in Christ over all the evil works of the enemy! Yes. It is never too late to be redeemed and restored in **every** area of your life!

Inform yourself that there is nothing wrong with you. You were not made wrong.
There was something wrong in you, not with you.

The God designed beautiful woman bases her life upon the truth of who God is and who she is. She knows Who made her, Who saved her, and Who is restoring her to the original magnificent divine design. She willingly submits to that awesome design.

As we embrace God's design, we are the women who excel as lovely and beautiful!

The worldly woman has nothing to compare with the beauty of holiness,

the radiance of unconditional, unfading love,
and the wisdom of Almighty God,
all wrapped up in a servant heart.

Discussion and Application

1. Reread the Genesis account in Chapters 1, 2, and 3.

2. Describe how and why God made the first woman.

3. Does your previous description of a woman's role agree or disagree with the Genesis account?

4. Read aloud Psalm 139: 13-1. How did God make you?

    Summarize the following in your own words:

   > *"For You formed my inward parts / You covered me in my mother's womb / I will praise You for I am fearfully and wonderfully made / Marvelous are Your works, / And that my soul knows very well. / My frame was not hidden from You / When I was made in secret / And skillfully wrought in the lowest parts of the earth / Your eyes saw my substance and being yet unformed / And in Your book they all were written / The days fashioned for me / When as yet there were none of them" (PS.139:13-16 NKJ).*

Can you recognize God as the Creator of your life as you read these lines?

5. Read through Psalm 139 and discuss the following:

   Commentary on Psalm.139: 1-6

   God knows you intimately. He is a very personal God. Verse 2 states that He is fully conversant with our lives whether we are resting or working. He knows our thoughts and plans. In verse 3 the Hebrew word *"comprehend"* means to sift or winnow. He sorts out both our words and thoughts, knowing what is wheat and what is chaff.This verse is also translated as "to count our steps" *"Does He not see my ways/ And count all my steps? (Job 14:16NKJ). "Does He not see my ways / And count my steps" (Job 31:4 NKJ)?* God knows our innocence. The reference to Psalm 56 also gives insight into His complete knowledge of us individually: *"You number my wanderings; / You put my tears into Your bottle; /Are they not in your book" (Ps.56:8 NKJ)?*

   David is certain that nothing he is going through is insignificant to God. God sees every tear that falls and lists them in His book, not one is lost. The person surrendered to God can know that every facet of life has meaning.

   Everything is recorded in God's Book of Remembrance, *"for those who fear the Lord /And who meditate on His Name."* . . .God listens and hears all that we say to one another. . .These who serve Him are His possession, *" They shall be Mine", says the Lord of Hosts/ On the day I make them My jewels. And I will spare them/As a man spares his own son who serves him"* (Mal 3:16b, 17 NKJ).

You are a beautiful jewel in the King's crown!

Verse 5 states that ***"You have hedged me behind and before /And laid Your Hand upon me."*** *"Hedged"* refers to enclosed. God has a protective blessing upon us. We are never out of His consciousness (Ps.40:5 NKJ).

6. How does God's blueprint for our lives differ from Satan's blueprint? Include the definition of functional representation.

Chapter 5

God's Divine Direction

However did I get to the Toronto Spirit-Led Conference in September of 2011? As stated in Psalm 139, God knows us intimately, and He certainly knew how I would assess the Conference. And He knew what would create the desire within me to attend that particular Prayer Conference. He is amazing. So here is the account of my Toronto Conference experience.

I had been watching Believers Voice of Victory on the Vision channel one morning and saw Terry Copeland Pearson inviting believers and partners of the Copeland Ministry to a Spirit-Led Prayer Conference. She said that the conference in Toronto was initiated by God. This was the first such Spirit Led Conference for Canada. The invitation tugged at my heart so I considered going. However, I needed the Lord to confirm if this was His will for me at that particular time. Weeks later I saw Terry Copeland Pearsons on the Believers Voice of Victory. She was holding a brochure with a picture of herself and a female speaker. To me, two women on the cover of a brochure meant that it was a Women's Prayer conference and I assumed it would be a rather small group. My interest was turning to excitement. The Lord knew that I would not be attracted to a large mixed group. He knew I would assume this would be a Women's Intercessory Prayer Conference which suited me just fine at my existing comfort level. I had no idea I would be attending a conference of a mixed group of 800 men and women!

Another confirmation other than the tug at my heart and the brochure was the fact that my husband would be in Toronto at the same time. That meant I could cut my hotel costs by sharing a room with him for the first 2 nights at a luxurious hotel. Things were coming together and before I knew it I was on a plane to the first Toronto Spirit-Led Conference for Canada. I knew God was leading me.

God knows the present, the past, and the future. He knew the marital inconvenience I would experience with my husband and that it would cause me to leave the hotel earlier than planned. That is exactly what happened. As I look back on the incident I realize that I would have preferred to be led by the Spirit for an earlier departure from the hotel. However at that time in my life, the unpleasant circumstance moved me and I learned the amazing reality that the Lord will use whatever will work to get us to where He wants us to go when we desire His will. He never coerces us but understands our circumstance and uses it for our good when we call upon His help. My husband would be attending his business meetings so I was free to use the time as I wanted and I wanted to go to the conference earlier than planned.

I was wearing my gym outfit and cross trainers, carrying a huge purse and heavy laden tote bag over my shoulders, pulling this over stuffed suitcase into the street to find the nearby subway. I love the determination to succeed. After lugging the suitcase over cobble stones and through heavy traffic I did find the right subway exit. I was at the right exit but I didn't know if I should be heading east or west to get to the Conference site. It was time for another prayer for help. Once again the Lord knew this would happen to me. A young man wearing earphones was stationed on the platform to direct me to the elevator for the eastbound subway. He said the Conference site was east! The Lord had placed people along the way to help me.

He directs our steps and He provides the help we need along the way.

The Conference hotel was located on the outskirts of Toronto. I was on the eastbound subway trusting Him to get me to my final destination. Besides the subway I would need to take a bus. Why did they ever arrange a conference on the outskirts of Toronto? When will I know where to get off the subway to catch the bus? Seated next to me was a very friendly woman who directed me when to get off the subway in order to catch the bus. Then she escorted me to the bus that was waiting on the platform. I was the last one to get on the bus - standing room only. I had just made it!

As I stood in the front aisle beside the bus driver, it didn't take long to discover that he was my brother-in-Christ. What a sweet wonderful young man. As we chatted with each other, a young woman from Sri Lanka was listening to our conversation and overheard me talk about the Conference. She was standing at the front of the bus very near to my hanging onto the bus driver's seat! She approached me to ask if anyone could come to the conference. Still assuming that it was a Women's Conference I gladly encouraged her to come. She was delighted.

She then proceeded to tell me how her husband always picked her up from work for the past year and a half since they had moved to Toronto, but today she had a nudge to leave work early and take the bus home. I shared my story of how I was supposed to be at the hotel but had a NUDGE to leave early as well. Now we were both at the same place at the same time for her to hear about the conference. Her name is Christiana and what a lovely young Christian woman she is. Not only did we have a divine connection on the bus, but we were getting off the bus at the exact same spot! She lived a block and a half away from the conference hotel!

I can't express how encouraged and loved I felt at meeting Christiana. I really was being Spirit led to the Spirit Led Conference. I am right on track connecting with the person who needed me to be there at that time. It is just fabulous to follow the leading of the

Lord. He has always led me to others who are following Him. Never ever think that following the Lord is a lonely experience. Never! Loneliness comes with His leadership only because of the gap between you and those who are *not* following Him. He will always connect you with others in His time and in His way.

So here I am at the Conference hotel but the Conference site is about 15-20 minutes by car via the freeway. Well we all know that I don't have a car, and a taxi would cost more than $40.00 one way depending on traffic. What am I going to do? Well, "ask and it shall be given". I asked the Lord to provide a ride for me. When I left the lobby of the hotel there was a van parked right outside the hotel entrance exactly as I came out of the door to look for God's provision. The couple inside the car was from Chicago and they invited me to ride with them. I was on my way to the Women's' Spirit-Led Conference!

Hilarious to me now but at that time when I arrived at the Conference site (on a University Campus) I noticed men everywhere. Inside the dome I heard lively praise and worship songs where women **and** men were "lifting up holy hands." "Oh no! This can't be right." I came for the Women's' Prayer Conference. I would never have registered for the conference if I had not believed it was for women only. After all, I minister to women, with women, for women, and because of women. What am I doing here with all these men? I will fast forward to the end of the story.

I was full of praise and thankfulness to the Lord for getting me all the way to the outskirts of Toronto. Meeting Christiana and later spending time with both she and her husband at the conference and at their home, was such sweet fellowship. My younger sister and brother in Christ honored me like a mother and we worshipped and prayed together as one in the Spirit.

The time of solitude and worship I spent in my hotel room, the sister in Christ from Chicago who was looking for a friend, the provision of rides to the conference and then back to the airport, (I did not have to take the subway and bus!) and the dynamic, inspiring, and encouraging message and prayers of the Conference were life changing, reviving, and empowering, preparing me for the next season of my life.

Where would I be without Him? (Not at the Toronto Conference!!!)

Chapter 6

Identity Crisis

As I talked with my sister one late summer afternoon, I emphasized how important it is not to lose sight of our true identity once we find it. It took me a long time to find my authentic self. I stressed how critical it is to find out who we were created to be, and that our identity needs to remain fixed as we journey through the different stages of life. Even now I sense urgency in completing this book as I know that other women will not have to wait as long as I did before discovering the truth about their value and beauty.

My sister continued to listen intently as I talked about identity, and then I suddenly switched gears. I remembered a time when I had lost sight of my true identity in Christ; when my mind had focused on the trauma of what was happening to me. My sister wanted to hear more about this; about the time I lost sight of my true identity in Christ. I became very somber and quiet as I looked out toward the tall Evergreens and blue sky. I had no words to speak, only memories of the remorse and deep shame I had experienced when I had been overcome by fear, despair, and rage. She urged me to share that dreadful time of my life. She said that women will be able to identify with what I had experienced. There must be someone reading this book that needs to hear this.

I had been a very committed and externally vibrant Christian for many years but didn't know there were places in my heart that had not been redeemed, and wounds that had not been healed. I began remembering how completely helpless I was to change what had happened to me. . . betrayed by someone I had trusted. Betrayal can take on many different forms and many different degrees. Whether betrayal by a trusted confidante, a best friend, a spouse, a sister, a brother-in-Christ, a parent, etc. it is inevitable that you will experience some form in your lifetime. This particular betrayal was one that opened me up to all kinds of hidden wounds and fears deep inside of me.

As the magnitude of my reaction toward the betrayal increased, my coping mechanisms were in high gear wavering between fight and flight, mostly fight. It seemed like I was inside a deep black pit that just kept getting deeper and darker. Fear, shock, anger, jealousy, lust, and hatred surfaced in unbearable pain, and in devilish rage against the person who had betrayed me. I retaliated with shock and terror, forgetting all I had ever heard about forgiveness. **I just wanted the pain to stop by making the other person see the damage inflicted upon me and to make things right.**

At that time I did not know or understand that the person who hurt you is not the person to heal you.

I was out of the control of the Holy Spirit. Jesus was not Lord over my thoughts or my feelings and especially not over my will or my physical body. This was an area in my life that scared me more than ever. I was horrified and needed rescuing. I was completely unaware that my unredeemed sexuality of viewing myself as unwanted, devalued and sexual object was latent in that false image, and it was being used as a weapon against me. Because of this betrayal former feelings of shame, and devalue flooded over me as I recalled the incident over and over. I was filled with rage and negative conclusions about myself. I had felt this very same way when I was a preteen, the time my Dad had accused me of lying. He was in a rage, throwing a suitcase full of my clothes out of the house, and me along with it. I felt that same shame when he had accused me of being promiscuous when I was in grade nine. It wasn't true but his accusation made me believe that he viewed me that way – as a "bad girl." Even though this circumstance of betrayal was different and so very many years had passed, the devastating thoughts and intense feelings of shame, hurt and fear were the same ones I felt as a young girl. I had forgiven my Dad later in life and we were reconciled so why did these feelings resurface?

Without a redeemed sexuality I was reacting out of the wrong, fallen image of womanhood.

I still believed lies about myself and had little if any understanding of the wrongs of others.

Early in life I *unconsciously* labeled myself with a "bad girl" image, mainly because of being spoken to that way by my Dad. Apparently other people said I was a bad little girl according to what my Mom had told me. And little boys would be mean to me without cause. Deep down I felt so much shame, and that shame made me feel very unsure of myself, especially as a valuable highly esteemed woman. I didn't know that I needed Christ's redemption in the area of my sexuality. I still lived out of the fallen image of an untrustworthy disapproved of bad girl who is objectified. This fallen wrong image of Satan's blueprint was marred by *habitual sinful patterns and controlled by demonic powers.* Even though I had been born-again in my spirit, baptized with the Holy Spirit and baptized in water, I needed redemption in my soul and body.

Verbal and physical abuse creates a rock solid foundational belief in the wrong image!

That foundational belief was based on a lie that produced shame, guilt and fear.

The lie had never been exposed, rejected and put to death. Only the truth would set me free!

I didn't have any understanding of why I was so out of control at that betrayal. Why did I feel so utterly helpless and desperate? Why couldn't I swallow without a lump in my throat and tension throughout my whole body? I felt as though I was left in the dark all alone. I couldn't understand how a grown woman in Christ could think and feel this way. I'm a new creation in Christ and old things have passed away and I have become new. What's happening to me? How can a grown woman in Christ think and behave like this? That old false image had been more real to me than my new true image in Christ? HELP!

Romans 7 and 8 tell us that when a believer walks in rebellion and sins against the nature and commands of God, the Holy Spirit experiences grief. The unconfessed sin creates a sudden loss of intimacy with this person whom the Holy Spirit loves. At that terrible time in my life, I had interrupted intimacy with the Holy Spirit the third **Person** of the Godhead. He, like God the Father and Creator, has personhood. My loss of connection with the Person of Holy Spirit produced grief in Him which lasted over a period of months.

Read Ephesians 4: 25-32 and you will notice some of the specific behaviors that cause the Spirit to grieve. These indications of how we treat others grieve the Spirit and disconnect us from intimacy: *lying, angry outbursts, stealing, corrupt speech, bitterness, wrath, clamor, evil speaking and malice.* It doesn't matter how long you have been a Christian. These behaviors can exert control over you when you do not have a strong identity as the *risen, empowered, and beautiful to the core daughter of the King*! Praise God that intimacy is always restored with repentance.

I gave in to all the temptations of fear. I could not resist the ugly and harmful thoughts and emotions that rose up from a place of darkness, a place in my heart that needed redemption and healing. I was cooperating with the devil himself- with his lies and the toxic deadly emotions that characterize his wicked nature. You may have heard that it's just our human nature to behave badly, or that we're just being human if we harbor a grudge, especially toward those people, or nations for that matter, who use or abuse us; that we have a right to demand recourse for their actions and to inflict punishment if necessary. Maybe you believe that we have a right to our pound of flesh-that somebody needs to pay for the injustice! After all it's only fair. My response to all the "injustice" and betrayal was anything but Christ-like. I became vindictive, full of the desire to make things right any way I could. My resentment and unforgiveness grew into bitterness, and my bitterness turned to hostility and rage toward the person who had betrayed me.

I had grieved the Holy Spirit and was out of intimate communication with Him.

I didn't realize it, but I was cooperating with the devil who is the master of all those ugly emotions. I have heard it said that *fully engaging in* destructive emotions such as these is like, "Having intercourse with the devil!" Yikes!

In all this turmoil and crisis, and in the midst of desperation and condemnation, the wrong image of my sexuality was exposed. God was working in this mess to free me from that wrong image and my unredeemed sexuality. His will was to free me from the lies I had unknowingly believed about myself since I was a young girl! Praise God! Yes, the Lord will take that which is meant for evil and turn it for our good and His glory when we yield to Him and His purposes. *And that is what happened when I finally gave up control over trying to make things right my way.*

I admitted that I couldn't make anything right -not even myself!

The Bible clearly states that what is meant for evil can be turned for good when we trust the Lord for His help and yield to His purposes (Rom.8:28 ELB). That is exactly what happened. The question of my true identity, value, and self-acceptance, became my primary concern. I didn't want to feel condemned and guilty, ashamed, unforgivable, and ugly any longer.

Where is the true worth and
beauty promised me in Christ?

I must have it!

I must return to the arms of a loving Savior Who
will forgive me, deliver me, heal me, and restore
me to His beautiful image!

Revelation and Insight Regarding Personal Crisis and Trauma

- Unknowingly I had believed lies about myself since childhood and had formed unconscious negative conclusions about myself based on those lies.
- I also had false assumptions about others and about God as well.

My subconscious held the false image
and Satan's blueprint.

Some of the hidden labels of that false image were "sex object", "unwanted" "foolish", "bad girl." Early in life these lies were deposited into my memory bank and into my subconscious. This false image was a silent killer of what I had been told to believe about myself as a new creation. This false image was a silent killer of the truth of the Word of God because I believed it! This old subconscious false image or blueprint had been there long before I knew of the true image.

At times it seemed that I wasn't consciously choosing to sin, but rather I was falling into a repeated pattern of sinful behavior. That repeated reaction produced a stronghold in my life. When deeply offended by perceived unfair treatment or injustice, I would experience automatic ungodly thoughts of hatred. These ungodly thoughts emerged to the surface at times with uncontrolled anger. "I don't deserve this. It's totally unfair. Why I am not treated with respect and kindness? I hate this kind of undeserved treatment."

The negative conclusion lodged in my subconscious was that I believed I must be unworthy of respect and kindness or else I would be receiving respect and kindness. I must not be of value or importance. I am insignificant, shameful, not wanted. Shame had done its damage in my life. The feelings of self-hatred, self-rejection, and guilt deeply hidden for years in my subconscious were being exposed.

No one told me about the power of my subconscious to "sabotage" my true identity!

Victim mentality does not belong to the true image in Christ. Being mistreated and devalued does not mean that you are worthless, bad or unwanted. Injustice does not make the victim of less worth. Victims may just conclude that they are of less worth, powerless, and bad. It's all my fault, I would think. If I would just love like Christ I wouldn't need to suffer this humiliation and rejection. I somehow believed that if I loved people like Christ, they would love me back; that it was up to me (not Christ) to get the love I wanted. I was living in the loving efforts of my flesh not in the power of the Spirit.

Although I was born again of the Spirit of God, my unrenewed mind, will, and emotions had been cooperating with the evil one! Yes he is the one whose nature is filled with all that is wrong and bad. Satan had a stronghold in me of that false image and he was determined to keep me in bondage. I am forever grateful that Jesus set me free.

To have a secure identity in Christ you must know to whom you belong, as well as knowing to whom you do not belong.

The truth is that I no longer belonged to the devil but I had entered into his domain of darkness and deception. How did I do that? When I took matters into my own hands I stepped outside the authority of God. I rejected God's authority over my life. Remember that the first sin ever committed by Eve was her acting independently of God? I needed to declare Christ's ownership over every part of me, and it would be the truth of Who Christ is and what He has done for me, and in me, that would set me free! "He heals the broken-hearted and sets the captives free" (Isa.61:1; Luke 4:18 ElB).

My sinful thoughts, feelings and behavior revealed that I was living in the false image.

I wish someone would have told me this and spared me the terrible condemnation and judgment I experienced.

I was rejecting myself on a subconscious level rather than accepting myself I was not loving myself as God's precious daughter. You may be doing the very same thing for the same reasons!

I began to grieve over the loss of all the years I had been in such darkness. I needed forgiveness for choosing to allow my sinful thoughts and reactions to rule over me, giving Satan control. I needed forgiveness for giving in to temptation, for being completely overcome at times with vindictive self-righteous anger. I needed to forgive myself as Christ forgives me, and then forgive the one who had betrayed me.

I had a battle going on within me that I really didn't know about or understand. Now I realize that God's desire was to bring me deliverance from the wrong image and replace that with His new one; one that represented His love and power. He only needed my cooperation in receiving His mercy and forgiveness. Then I was able to extend that same mercy and forgiveness to those who had caused such pain in my life. You can see that becoming a Christian is only the first step to living a new life. There is so much more to learn about that new life as a daughter of the King!

Without forgiveness there would be no control of the Spirit and consequently no healing for all the wounds of the past. I had grieved over my sinfulness and now I needed to receive forgiveness toward myself- just the way Christ had already forgiven me on the cross. What a weight was lifted as I cried tears of repentance. I sensed His love wash over me in forgiving me all my sinning. Then I released that gracious loving merciful forgiveness to the one who had betrayed me.

I no longer believed the ugly lies about myself.

I received God's love for me as His beautiful forgiven daughter.

Consequences of Living in the Wrong Image

We are either mastered by our selfish and sinful wrong image, which places us under the control of Satan, or we are mastered by the selfless new image of Christ, which is under the control of God through His Holy Spirit. A controlling root of addiction and compulsive behavior is buried in that sinful wrong image.

We have many influences and voices that speak to us, but we only have to choose one nature – either that of godliness or ungodliness; the nature of God or the nature of Satan. Pretty shocking isn't it?

We cannot have two natures functioning simultaneously!

In Christ we have a new nature, made in the image of God's character.

This is the true image of the beautiful woman.

In Christ we have been given everything that pertains to life and godliness (2Pet.1:3, 4 ELB). We are partakers of the divine nature and "co-heirs" with Christ, designed to rule over creation and subdue all things unto God. Wholeheartedly we are growing more beautiful every day.

Discussion and Application

1. Do you believe things about yourself that aren't true? Have these negative conclusions based on lies influenced your foundational beliefs? What is the truth from the Word of God?

2. Can you remember those things that were said about you in your childhood and/or in your adolescence that became labels?

3. Did you label yourself unconsciously or knowingly? Why?

4. Has the worldly view of women influenced your self image? How?

5. Are women of the world usually portrayed as seductive, devious, and manipulative? As having it all?

6. After a Christian Women's Retreat one young woman commented that before she came to Christ, she dressed "to seduce men and to intimidate women". Can you identify with this false image in any way?

   • How has the image of a Christian woman missed the mark?

   • Have we been painted as servile, self-righteous and judgmental?

   • How does the world in general view the Christian woman?

7. How have you been viewed by others as a Christian woman?

8. Ask the Holy Spirit to reveal any wrong conclusions or beliefs you may still have that do not belong to your new identity

in Christ. Choose to discard those and replace them with the truth(s) you have discovered.

9. Do you believe that your true image and identity is created by the character of God in Christ? Why is that true?

10. Have you experienced a redeemed sexuality?

Chapter 7

Risen, Empowered, and Beautiful to the Core

Powerful Truths

Our true identity in Christ is the answer to all our self-doubt and quest for fulfillment, no matter what age or stage of life.

It is out of our true identity we are able to function individually, and collectively, in the blueprint God has designed for us.

"He gave me beauty for ashes, the oil of joy for mourning, a garment of praise for a spirit of heaviness, so that I would be a tree of righteousness, the planting of the Lord, that He would be glorified" (Isa.61:3 NKJ).

My fallen false image needed to be redeemed and redefined. I would be free to see myself as the risen, empowered, and beautiful to the core daughter of the King! Likewise, you are set free from Satan's blueprint, for the same purpose.

John Eldridge in his book <u>Journey of Desire</u> declares that mankind was created for pleasure, that his beginning and end is a paradise and that the goal of living is to find Life. Jesus knows that ecstasy is not an option; we are made for bliss, and we must have it one way or another. All the Christian disciplines were formulated at one time or another in an attempt to heal our desire's waywardness and so, by means of obedience, bring us home to bliss. The goal, Eldridge states, is ecstasy, and this makes us beautiful!

Who can deny the beauty of a woman in love*?*

A life of obedience to God brings us bliss.

And this gives us honor! As we honor the Lord with our beautiful lives, He honors us in ways that we could never think or even imagine. How can we ever thank Him enough?

You Are Risen

You are "risen in Christ." Read Colossians 2: 6-14. "Risen" is equated with new life. You are resurrected from the death of your sinful nature. You have chosen to die to your old sinful self to live a new resurrected life each day as the righteousness of God in Christ Jesus. It is the exchange of an old life for a new life- a false image exchanged for the true image. You have risen to a new way of thinking, feeling, and behaving. As your mind becomes renewed with the mind of God, the truth of His Word washes away the old thought patterns, replacing them with new ways of thinking and perceiving. You are being transformed into the nature of God in Christ. Your old sinful nature has been crucified with Christ by faith and now it is no longer you in that old fallen state that exists, but it is a new risen you, living as a "co-heir and co-laborer with Christ. *"It is no longer I who lives but Christ lives in me" (Gal.2:20 NIV).*

"Risen" in the new life and nature of Christ gives us fellowship with God and with each other. Close loving and honest communication with The Lord and with each other draws us to completeness and unity. *"If we walk in the light as He is in the Light then we have fellowship one with another" (JN.1:7 NIV).* The "Light" is another word for the truth.

You are "Empowered"

Read Colossians 2:15; Luke 10:19. We are **"empowered by His grace."** It is not that your old self has been worked on and improved that brings you the power to live an abundant Life. It is in the humility of receiving God's forgiveness and grace that gives you the ability to become a totally new creation. His grace is sufficient for all things that pertain to your godliness! That is what enables you to live the abundant life.

*He will do for you and in you
what you cannot do for yourself.*

That which is flesh cannot inherit His Kingdom.

His grace is all-sufficient! We have been given authority in and by Christ over all the works of the flesh and we have been given His authority and victory over all the works of the devil. When we believe this truth we can choose to say "no" to both.

Our will is influenced by the truth that we have died with Christ, crucifying the power of our flesh to control us (carnal appetites and desires), nullifying Satan's nature and control over us.

Our will follows whatever is strongest in us!

We have not been given authority or control over each other. We are given authority over the earth, the flesh and the devil! Our delegated authority comes from God in and through Christ. You are seated with Christ far above all evil powers and principalities, being given the authority to reign in Christ over them, with Him. I have inherited authority and ownership (Matt.16:17-19 NIV).

"I will give you the keys of the Kingdom of heaven; and whatever you bind (declare to be improper and unlawful) on earth, must be what is already bound in heaven; and whatever you loose (declare lawful) on earth must be what is already loosed in heaven" (Matt.16:19; Isa.22:22 NIV).

Because His Spirit and His Word are within us we can know what God's will is on earth as it is in heaven. We have authority on earth to bring heaven's will into action. What is bound and loosed in heaven – what He allows or disallows- is that which we have the authority to allow or disallow here in the earth.

Empowerment also involves taking personal responsibility and owning your own problems.

Be empowered by giving up a competitive spirit. This does not make you a wimp or a fool. It actually takes more strength to treat others well in face of mistreatment or neglect. The stronger woman shows kindness to those who mistreat her. Kindness is a language the dumb can speak and the deaf can hear and understand!

We have been given this grace to treat others better than they deserve to be treated. Those who are least deserving, need God's love the most! How merciful is our God? Give up your rights and you will stop demanding justice and fairness. A beautiful woman is full of His grace. She has repented of her own pride and preferences.

Also we are empowered to "suffer" according to the will of God which is *always redemptive* and will *always lead* to deep joy, satisfaction, and Christ- likeness. Suffering takes the form of denying your flesh the pleasures it desires, waiting for God's intervention when things look hopeless, and selflessly accepting what is difficult or seemingly impossible to endure. Therefore pray to be strengthened to do God's will - to choose the excellent way, the high road, and to choose to have every kind of endurance and patience, with the joy of the Lord. He is bigger than anything you will ever need to endure. Praise and adore Him for it!

Suffering according to God's will always leads to deep joy, satisfaction, and Christ-likeness.

You are "Beautiful to the Core"

Being born of the incorruptible seed of the Word of God makes you altogether perfectly beautiful and complete in the image of God in Christ. The spiritual seed of the life of Christ has been planted deep within at the very core of your being. Christ and the seed Word are the same. All of godliness is within that seed. And the love of God has been shed abroad in your heart by the Holy

Spirit within this seed. This seed needs to grow to maturity into the likeness and love of our Lord Jesus Christ. This image of God in Christ is at your very core in seed form. As you water this seed with the truth of the Word of God and nurture it with the sunshine of the love God has for you, the transforming power of the Holy Spirit produces the beauty of the fruit of the spirit.

Your feminine heart is restored in its true form; you are truly beautiful, truly alive, and truly you!

You are able to experience a love beyond all measure.

There is nothing more beautiful than a woman in love!

Society sends the message that you need to *attract* love by:

- popularity
- sex appeal
- physical appearance
- performance

These are not God's standards.

Sometimes it seems that a local church or denomination may stress the same things as listed above - that we as Christians need to attract the world with our Christianity. Christ did not come to earth to attract the world. He came to forgive and to sacrifice Himself for the world (Jn.3"16 NKJ).

We all need to learn how to give love rather than straining and striving to attract it!

You will become skilled and filled in the art of loving. Giving love is inherent in the beauty of godliness, and godliness is perfected by abiding in the Vine.

"I am the vine, you are the branches. Whoever lives in Me and I in him bears much (abundant) fruit." (Jn.15:5 ELB). The definition for "abide" is to remain, continue, dwell; remain faithful to; obedience. Mostly it means to have **unbroken** fellowship/friendship with Jesus.

Is it possible that if I don't learn to know truth by the revelation of the Word of God, and learn to hear what the Spirit is saying, I'll walk the old way according to the fallen image of Satan's blueprint and the results will be disastrous?

The biblical answer is found in the parable of sowing and reaping. ***"We reap what we sow" (Gal.6; 7-9 NKJ).*** We either sow to the flesh and its desires or we can sow to the spirit. The Word of God feeds our spirit! Remember that the desires of our flesh (sinful nature) are *always* contrary to the desires of the spirit; ". . .fleshly lusts war against our soul" (1Pet. 2:11 NKJ).

"Flesh" referred to here is the whole of human nature in alienation from God: pride, selfishness, the drive for power, overindulgence. You could think of flesh as the unredeemed entire self. And we know that the flesh and the Spirit are in constant contention for supremacy (Rom.7 & 8 NKJ).

Who will you choose to rule over you?

An intimate relationship with Christ and this new way of Life is nurtured by sowing to the spirit, and abiding in the vine.

We learn and practice how to abide in the Vine. Jesus is the Vine and we are the branches! Just picture a vine with sap flowing throw its branches. That's Holy Spirit sap flowing through those branches. Yes, we are the branches attached to the Vine. We literally nourish one another as we stay connected to and flow with the sap of the Spirit from the Vine. We learn to consistently sow to the Spirit by keeping that vital relationship of intimacy with Jesus number one in our life. We always need to stay close to Jesus sensing His love and purposes, following Him by His side in His Word. It is so easy to attend Church services and events without flowing in the sap of the Spirit, referred to as the anointing. It will become evident if your branch is becoming dry and is not bearing the fruit of the Spirit.

Review Galatians 5 to see if you are bearing the fruit of the Spirit or the fruit of the flesh.

John 15:1-8 tells us that God prunes us and cuts away things that no longer bear the fruits of righteousness. This "cutting away" is often painful, as we abide in the vine, but necessary to produce the fruit of the Spirit. Abiding in the Vine yields much fruit.

Abiding in Christ brings lasting joy and gladness of heart.

In Galatians: 5:22, Paul lists the fruit of the Spirit. Yes, the fruit of the Spirit is greater than the lusts of our flesh. Believe it! Don't allow the devil to deceive you into believing the lie that your flesh is stronger than your spirit even though that's how it feels. The five senses are natural and deceiving. Your own heart and emotions can and will deceive you. In Christ we have all the authority over our flesh and every evil power that would attack us in spirit, soul, body, relationships, and in every other aspect of our lives. We have new kingdom authority over our flesh, worldliness, and the devil, which has been delegated to us by Christ. Now use it!

The character of God in Christ is our new nature.
The power of Satan's character and blueprint has
been exposed and broken. As Jesus is so are you!
Amazing.
Trust the truth and the Spirit in you.

New Identity as God's Daughter and Representative

You will need to know how to dress and conduct yourself in the role God has designed and ordained for you. The image you project to others can be very confusing to the vision that God has for you, if you forget who and whose you are. The world's image of beauty and power is portrayed in a sensuous and sexual fountain of youth. Women of all ages try to hang on to their youth, forgetting that God designed us to be *youthful* not young indefinitely.

Women desperately grasp at holding onto their outward youth, not realizing that they have been made eternal! The latest advancement in anti-aging cosmetics, plastic surgery, and power exercising only works on "beautifying" the outside. Comparing yourself to worldly "beauty" is part of that fleshly fallen nature- that false image. Look into the mirror of God's Word to find out who you really are, not into the mirror on the wall!

God's image of beauty and power
come from the inside out.

NB *The image you behold is the image you become.*

We are to compare ourselves to Christ, and not to one another, and certainly not to Hollywood! Your new nature will transform your "old" soul and body. We all need to go to God's beauty school!

As we know Him for who He really is, we will get to know ourselves as we really are. . . risen, empowered, and beautiful to the core. . .created in His image.

As we continue to look upon Jesus we will see a reflection of ourselves in Him, and then we become His reflection. Amazing!

Discussion and Application

1. What does it mean to be "risen, empowered, and beautiful to the core"? *have a clean heart! PEACE*
2. In what ways have you recognized yourself "risen" in Christ?
3. How do you receive "power" to live the Christian life? *prayer*
4. What does God call "beautiful"? Give scriptural references.

a clean heart & a peaceful heart

5. How does the following admonition "beautify" a woman?

    live life by pleasing Jesus in His will .

    ". . .keep your tongue from evil. . . do not repay evil with evil. . . but bless. Who is going to harm you if you are eager to do good?" (1Pet.3:9 ELB). *no one!*

6. Read John 15: 1-9. Why is abiding in the vine so critical?

7. How will you dress and conduct yourself to project this new vision of being God's representation on earth?

    Stay close to Jesus!
    Dress carefully " wise".

Chapter 8

New Perspective

In Christ you are not seductive, controlling, foolish or manipulative. You have not been redeemed to be servile, self-righteous, or judgmental. As a born-again daughter of the King, you are "risen, empowered, and beautiful to the core."

Let God redefine and refine who you are.

The image you behold is the image you become!

As we continue to look upon Jesus we will see a reflection of ourselves in Him, and then we become His reflection!

You are a beautiful woman created in the image of God and a daughter of the King, highly prized, loved, honored, and cherished, gifted and enabled with strength and wisdom. You are seated with

Christ high above all the evil powers and principalities. . . (Eph 1:20-21, NKJ)

Christ has implanted His nature within you!

Remember that as Jesus is, so are you.
Start to view yourself this way.
Begin to treat yourself with all the high esteem
that Christ has bestowed upon you, and then treat
others even better than yourself. . . especially
when they do not deserve it!
Amazing!

Look in the mirror of God's Word and see that the character and ability of Christ is in you. You are His divine design and His great love for you and in you, is continuing to perfect and establish you in His image. His love for you is completely and everlasting unconditional. You are His workmanship, magnificently crafted and marvelous to behold. Everything pertaining to godliness has been implanted in you (2 Peter 1:5, NKJ). Don't let the devil deceive you into believing you still belong to your old unredeemed nature. Jesus has set you free to be His beloved. In humility receive His grace that enables you to do what you cannot do without Him. The good work He has begun in you He will complete (Philippians 1:6, **NKJ**).

Positionally, we will always remain in Christ as daughters of the King. However, we can still *function*, *think* and *feel more* as a daughter who is fallen, defeated, and unattractive. Remember that when we fail, our position has not changed; we do not lose our position as God's beloved daughter, even though we have behaved badly, out of harmony with our new creation image. If our thoughts are wrong (out of alignment with God's truth), identity becomes blurred, and our senses will take over. When this happens, we demonstrate the fruit of the flesh, characterizing Satan rather than reflecting Jesus. HELP!

Can you think of a particular "mood" you entertain?

Do you ever feel self-pity or intense anger rising within you?

Do you carry a load of cares?

Simply run to Jesus and tell Him *all* about it! Tell Him about the bad mood, the uncontrolled anger, the worries and cares, and you will recognize it as the sin of that old blueprint which can so easily grab hold of your thoughts and emotions. Give them all to Jesus and receive His love and forgiveness upon your honest confession. Too often we carry these pent up emotions within us and enter into Satan's domain.

These lyrics from the famous hymn entitled <u>What a Friend We Have in Jesus</u> help us to unload everything on Jesus.

"What a friend we have in Jesus
All our sins and griefs to bear.

What a privilege to carry
Everything to God in prayer.
Oh what peace we often forfeit
Oh what needless pain we bear.
All because we do not carry
Everything to God in prayer."

The truth you can easily forget is that destructive feelings and habitual patterns don't have power to control you any longer unless you believe they reflect who you are. Jealousy, rage, and resentment are no longer part of your new person. The power of these sinful destructive feelings to control you has been broken. They do not belong to your new nature in Christ. Simply confess and repent of believing the lie that these destructive emotions reveal the real you. They are part of the old identity- the fallen nature. Keep training your mind to believe the truth and you will keep rejecting and releasing all those lying destructive and negative feelings to Jesus.

How are you thinking?

The devil will bring condemnation on you for these negative feelings and thoughts. He wants to trap you into believing that you have not been set free from their power to rule you. Run to King Jesus beautiful princess! On bended knee, confess wrong believing and any wrong doing, and ask for His forgiveness. He is faithful to forgive you and to cleanse you of all unrighteousness *(*1 John1:5-9 NKJ*)*.Amen.

The truth of who we are in Christ does not change when we fail or sin.
The forgiveness of Christ upon confession, cleanses us daily from anything that does not belong to our new identity.
A beautiful woman is not perfect.

While you are on your knees it's a good habit to ask the Lord to search your heart for any hidden hurt or wrong beliefs, or any negative conclusions you may have about yourself or about others. **The Holy Spirit reveals the truth about Jesus and about you!**

- Ask Him how you are currently viewing yourself and others.
- Ask Him to show you the root of any hidden sin. ***"He is faithful and just to forgive us our sins and to cleanse us from all unrighteousness" (1 John 1:9) NKJ.*** It is for freedom that he sets you free from all wrong and all harm. Remember that when you sin, *you do not need to be punished. You need to be forgiven!*
- We can ask for the grace of repentance for believing a lie about ourselves, about others, or about God, and then we can reject anything that is contrary to God's character and

ways. *That which is contrary to God's ways and character belongs to the fallen false image!* That false image has no power over your thoughts, feelings or conduct unless you believe it does. The devil and his blueprint for your life have been defeated. This is the truth, and it is the truth that sets you free. Amen?

- The Lord will lift you up in His strong loving arms of forgiveness and grace. Only Christ and Christ alone is our source of forgiveness and restoration. As we bow before Him in humility with a contrite heart, the light of His countenance will shine upon us and give us peace, joy, and renewed vision.
- Thank Him for such faithfulness, kindness, mercy, and love.

Any type of wrong image and label you have had of yourself must be rejected, as often as it reappears! My subconscious image as unwanted, sex object, bad girl, insecure, and foolish, was exposed and I needed to reject all of these labels. They did not belong to my new identity in Christ. They do not reflect the real me. However, during times of great trial or pain in my life circumstances, the devil would remind me of my past. It was at those times I needed to rebuke the devil and his spirit of condemnation, confessing who I am in Christ. The past is over, forgiven, and will be completely forgotten! The Bible tells us to put off (reject the lies of the past) of the old man with all its lust and corruption (Col 3, ELB). Jesus our Lord and Savior, Who is the Lover of Our Soul, wants our soul to be filled with His Goodness and Likeness. Behavior will be changed with *established true redeemed identity*. The more we know and embrace our true identity, the more our soul and body will reflect it!

We must reject the old to embrace the new!

I embrace the truth that I am highly prized and valued, deeply loved, and the object of God's affection, filled with His goodness and wisdom.
Yes I am made in God's image and crowned with glory and power (Ps. 8, ELB)

This is who I am. This is who I want to be!

How about you?

Can you repeat the quoted scripture out loud and believe it with all your heart?

Longing for Love

What I am about to tell you has set many women free. This freedom belongs to you! When we as women have been deceived we don't even know we are living a lie. Believing a lie produces bondage. That was definitely true in my life. I was deceived and I didn't know it. It was much later in my Christian life, through the study of God's Word, that I discovered something that shocked me. I had unknowingly been living under a curse. That curse was the consequence or result of Eve's (*unintentional*) sinning against the command of God. This resulting curse caused unredeemed, disconnected woman, to desire and intensely long for a relationship with a man, more than desiring and longing for that intimacy in relationship with God. Desiring a relationship with a man would become almost an obsession. Woman would be told she is incomplete without a man in her life.

The Bible lets us know that we are "complete in Him." How many movies, books, magazines, and other forms of media tell you that you are not complete unless you have a man? The message of the world says that you need someone or something you don't have. The truth is that you are incomplete when you do not have a relationship with God your Creator and Lover of your soul.

When you experience relationship with God the Father, God the Son, and God the Holy Spirit you become whole. Without this intimacy and competeness, you will live in fear or frustration of not having what you want or think you need. This is where deception enters your mind. Believing that you need someone else to make you complete will lead you to desire, demand, or manipulate within the male-female relationship out of that fear of not having what you think you need. This opens your life to demonic influence.

We must renounce believing that a relationship with a man will meet all our needs- particularly all our emotional needs. We can receive forgiveness for this and gain a new perspective. We can embrace the truth that in Christ, all our needs are met. All our longings will then be directed to a love relationship with Him. He is the Bridegroom and we are His Bride! What freedom women have experienced because of the realization (including myself of course) of misplaced longings for love. When you are free to be complete in Christ you can enjoy a different and new healthy relationship with a man. . . and with others, including yourself.

It makes no difference if you are single or married; you will be under this curse of longing and desiring a relationship with a man more than desiring and longing after God. You can reject the curse by recognizing Christ's sacrifice that broke its power. As a born-again, redeemed, daughter of the King, you are designed to live under the blessing not under this curse!

Regarding Marriage

Christian marriage is designed to be a representation of the relationship between Christ and His Church. The wife represents the Bride (the Church) and the husband represents the Bridegroom (Christ). Do you know what type of relationship Christ has with His church? How does He want us to view Him? What is His view of us?

How we *regard* our husbands will reflect how we regard our God! This was a hard pill for me to swallow! I didn't understand that "regard" meant how I viewed him, not how I *reacted* to him. I needed to take a closer look at this correlation and how I regarded my husband. Repentance is my middle name!

Wives are to reverence their husbands as unto the Lord, and husbands are to love their wives as Christ loves the church and gave His life for her (Ephesians 5:25, **NKJ**). We only need to concern ourselves with our role and calling as godly wives, and I'm still endeavoring to keep working on my part!

The husband is the head of the wife and the head of the husband is Christ (Ephesians 5:23, NKJ).

Headship is characteristic of sacrificial love and humble leadership.
Headship does not mean domination; submission does not mean "Do what you're told."

Order is essential to God's kingdom, not domination, and so He has chosen to create marriage and family with positions and protections of authority according to the way He has designed us to function. Submission of the wife to the husband's **position and authority** will give her **a safe and protected place from the enemy of her soul and marriage; even if her husband is wrong or carnal!** How I wish I knew this when I was first married. Refusing to yield to our husband's God given authority under Christ will allow the enemy access to our lives and marriages. A demonic spirit described as

Jezebel will become active in manipulation of the husband's role as spiritual head in the marriage, and the woman will be deceived into believing she has spiritual discernment to over-ride her husband's decisions. Does this sound familiar to anyone out there?

How I needed to understand what submission really meant. Dr. Larry Crabb studied its origin and definition and according to his research, the word submission in its biblical context *does not mean "Do what you're told." Rather it means to arrange yourself to a larger pattern- to get into formation in order to advance the purposes of God by yielding to authority.* This releases His power to work *in those to whom we submit,* as unto the Lord. Now that is much different than being a doormat. **Submission to the husband's God given position to advance the purposes of God brings a win -win situation to both of you. I believe this can only be done honestly as you continually are yielded in submission to the Lord, trusting God's design for marriage.** Not submitting would be comparable to a *rebellious cancer inhibiting good health in the entire body.*

Can you identify with the havoc in your marriage because of power struggles, misunderstanding and miscommunication, all of which produce offense, pain, distrust and despair, to name a few?

Submission to the husband's authority (whether he is godly or not) is supported and endorsed by God Himself.

This does not mean you cannot have your own opinion or disagree with your husband in a godly manner. Your feedback and perspective may be just what he needs.

Yes, in order for marriage to be restored to its true image husbands and wives are refined and tested in the fires of affliction . . ."made new by suffering"(Isaiah 48:10(ELB). Marriage certainly is the place for the fires of affliction. However as we are tried and tested, our faith can become as pure gold! We are made new in character and increased in faith as we become empowered by his grace, in this beautiful transformation.

Empower a woman and you empower a household. Empower a household and you empower a community. Amen!

Remember that the true definition of submission is to arrange yourself and yield to fit into a larger pattern- to get into formation to advance the purposes of God.

"Lord keep helping me to that end!"

A mighty releasing of God's grace and mercy will flood our lives as we trust Him with our husbands. He will even change *our* hearts! Let's ask Him for the grace of repentance and whole-hearted forgiveness for everything that went wrong. Cast your utter help-lessness to change others (and yourself) upon the Lord for He cares more about change than we do. He wants to change us, and only *He* can transform us to become more and more like Himself.

We can choose to either grow up or give up.
That sinful nature (resembling the devil) has been
crucified with Christ at the cross. That means
that Satan's power over us and our marriages has
been broken.

Believe it! The power of Christ's sacrificial blood has given you forgiveness and freedom to live in obedience and submission. It just takes practice! Ouch!

With every choice of obedience we make, we add
another nail in the coffin of that former unre-
deemed woman.
Bury her deep down and out of sight and sound!

The power of sin and Satan has been defeated and we have been given authority over our flesh, the devil, and worldliness (not over our husbands!). It's time to get out your hammer and put another nail in that coffin. Christian marriage will give you more than enough opportunity to do so. Let's inspire change in each other as godly women and wives.

Look beyond what you see; you are not being
defined by your past. Go through the fire of

refining. It is in the fire that you are being rede-
fined by your future!
I am forever grateful!

An excellent book on marriage that I highly recommend is The Politically Incorrect Wife by Nancy Cobb and Connie Grigsby.

Discussion and Application

1. Review the questions at the beginning of the chapter. Do you notice any similarities with each other? Have you defined yourself by your past or by your behavior?

2. Describe yourself as a new creation. Are you aiming for perfection?

3. What specifically has changed in the way you view yourself today?

4. What happens when you fail or sin?

5. Do you have a new perspective on submission? Can you put the definition in your own words and what that means for you practically?

6. In what ways does your marriage relationship reflect the relationship of Christ and His Bride?

7. Whether married or single, in what ways will you trust the Lord to make the necessary changes in you as His Bride?

Section II

Remember

Chapter 9

Strengthen and Reinforce your New Identity

Your new identity affects the relationship you experience with the Lord, and it affects the relationship you experience with yourself, and with others!

Strengthening and reinforcing your new identity is an on-going process which needs to become intentional.

Perspective and Purpose: What Am I Thinking?
Read Genesis 50: 15-21

- Joseph knew to whom he belonged and what he was called to do.

- Remembering his identity and purpose maintained his integrity.
- He knew His Father's heart was forgiveness and reconciliation toward his brothers.
- Joseph had God's perspective- knowing that God is faithful; what was meant for evil God would turn for his good and God's glory. Joseph's family, all of Egypt, and many peoples of the world would be blessed.
- He was willing to change and to trust God according to God's design and will for His life

It is so good to be reminded of the account of Joseph's life because we can understand God's perspective on our own life circumstances. God always looks at your heart condition more than anything else. He wants His daughters (and sons) to depend on Him and to trust Him with all their heart, not to lean on human understanding (Proverbs 3:4-6, NKJ). I have thought of Joseph often over the years. I remember how unjustly he was treated by his own brothers and by Potiphar's wife, and how the fellow prisoner who had promised to mention Joseph to the King completely ignored his promise and Joseph was forgotten for two more years. But God had not forgotten Joseph! I needed to be reminded of that when I felt forgotten and rejected (more than once!).

Remember that our Heavenly Father knows and cares about what we are going through and has a plan. He will work out all things in your life for good according to His purpose as you trust in Him and rely upon Him with your whole heart (Romans 8:28, ELB).

The world, your flesh, and the devil are not working for your good, but are working against your good. That's another reality! We can remind each other of this and then choose to believe the truth of God's love and purposes. Jeremiah tells us that the plans God has for you are for good and for a future and hope (Jeremiah 11, NKJ). You are not a victim, and you are not defined by your past, or your present circumstances. You are a daughter of the King. . . "risen, empowered, and beautiful to the core", whether you feel like it or not! And God *always* has a way for you where there seems to be no way.

> *How you continue to think about yourself, about God, and about others will give you a strong foundation for vision and purpose.*

You Have Position and Authority

First and foremost, everyday and every hour of the day, you need to remember who you are and to whom you belong, and to see yourself as the greatly beloved daughter of the King. You have a royal position and delegated authority from Christ. See yourself as a *warrior princess* who will fight the good fight of faith from a position of victory in and through Christ.

141

The word "authority" in the Greek (*"exousia"*) means the power of *delegated* right, mastery, or rule. It is different from the dunamis, which is the power of the authority of God inherent in God, to perform miracles, signs and wonders. Praise God that Satan has no legal right to rule over you any longer. You have "exousia" over him and his demonic host. Your sin debt has been paid in full and Jesus is your Lord and Savior. You know that your real enemy is Satan. He hates God and he hates you! People are not your enemy. People need Jesus and the love He offers. The evil spirit influencing or working through a person(s) is the real enemy. You have been given authority delegated by Christ over all the power of the enemy and all his evil ways (Luke 10:19, **NKJ**). You no longer belong to the darkness of deception; you have been translated into His Kingdom of the glorious Light of Truth. Meditate upon the *truth* and faith will rise in your heart.

Take a moment to remember and to reflect upon who you are and to Whom you belong. God says you are His daughter: a risen, empowered, and beautiful to the core, daughter of Creator Father God. He formed you – woman- out of deep love and desire for companionship with Himself with others. You belong to Him and not to this world or to the things of this world.

Don't believe that you are still the old fallen image of powerlessness and victimization. That gives you the wrong identity. In Christ, you are the one with authority over all the works of the Evil one, and the fruit of the Spirit has power over the sinful works of the flesh (Gal.5:16 NKJ). You are designed to function as a warrior princess!

"And I will give you the keys of the Kingdom of heaven and whatever you bind (declare to be improper and unlawful) on earth must be what is already bound in heaven; and whatever you loose (declare lawful) on earth must be what is already loosed in heaven" Matt.16:19 ELB). "I will place on his shoulder the key to the house of David; what he opens no one can shut, and what he shuts no one can open." (Isa.22:22 NIV)

Keys signify ownership and the authority to enter. Only the owner has a right to the keys of that place of ownership. As a born again believer you have been given the keys to His (spiritual) palace, His kingdom. You are His daughter and you live in His palace with His authority to rule by His Law of Agape love. You have been equipped to walk after the spirit not fulfilling the lusts of your fleshly desires.

Seeking first His kingdom means that you are seeking His reign and rule over your own life first!!!

The nature of God in Christ is being developed and perfected in you as you submit to His Lordship.

143

How can you possibly think of yourself as a victim, a weakling, helpless, or abandoned?

If you find yourself loving the things of this world you have not embraced the love of your Heavenly Father. God's love is the chain that binds the keys of the kingdom together. Open your heart and be filled with the love of God in Christ that is greater than the selfish desires of your flesh. Remember that you need to believe *that your sinful nature has been crucified on the cross of Christ. He died as you in your sinful human nature . . . defeating its power! You have been crucified with Christ, and you no longer live in that sinful nature, but in the nature of God in Christ. Amen! No* door will remain locked for you. You have entry to His kingdom riches. When you walk in the spirit, living your life controlled by the Holy Spirit, you will not be controlled by the desires of the sinful nature. Remember that you cannot have two natures functioning simultaneously! Speak with your delegated authority over the demands of your flesh and the temptations of the devil.

Living in His spiritual Kingdom governed by the Law of His Love, means you know that Jesus in you is greater than the devil in this world. Christ's sacrificial, forgiving and affirming deep love has more power than any selfish human love. It is Christ's victory over all darkness that causes you to believe that you now are able to live and walk in the Light as He is in the Light. No more do you believe the lies of darkness but you are living in the light of the truth of the

Word of God, declaring who you are and to whom you belong. You are a child of the Light. You are a daughter with delegated authority to rule and reign by the power of His law of agape love.

By faith you walk in the grace and humility of the God Who formed you.

Living in the power of the spirit keeps us in our kingdom authority. We learn to verbally declare (bind) that which is improper or unlawful just as it is in heaven, and we verbally declare lawful (loose) that which is allowed in heaven.

How do you know what to bind on earth and what to loose from heaven?

You know what to bind or loose by knowing God's will according to His written Word and the confirmation of the Holy Spirit. They never contradict one another. Whatever God does not allow in heaven, we bind on earth. Whatever is allowed in heaven we loose on earth. His kingdom come and His will be done on earth *as it is in heaven!* As His daughters and sons we are to *declare* His will on this earth.

When we follow after the flesh we cannot access the Kingdom's rule. We have entered Satan's domain and we cannot operate in our kingdom authority.

Satan is an offense, a hindrance and a snare to the Person and work of Christ, and he tempts us daily to enter into his domain and rule.

Satan uses devices against Christians and in Christians by deceiving their natural carnal mindset so that they do not think or act like the King.

Yes, Satan can inject a thought, a feeling, a mood, or a trigger within your mind or emotions. However, he cannot read your thoughts.

Keep remembering that!

A good example of this from the Word of God involves the disciple Peter. Peter was rebuked by Jesus when he told Jesus that he didn't need to go to the cross. Satan tells us the same thing; you don't need to follow the narrow path of obedience by suffering according to God's will; it's foolish and futile he shouts in our ears! Yet the truth is that obedience to God's will brings a suffering only of our flesh not getting its own selfish way, but blessings follow after the temporary trial. Remember that suffering according to the will of God is always redemptive.

Rebuke the devil when He tells you that you don't need to follow the narrow road of obedience to the cross.

Reject the carnal words, thoughts and/or actions which are contrary to the character and ways of God and the Kingdom mindset.

Jesus said to Peter "Get behind me Satan. . . for you are minding what partakes not of the nature and quality of God, but of men" (Matt. 16:23 ELB).

Those are the words of Jesus and we must remember that Christ by His Holy Spirit lives in us to rebuke the devil whenever required! Jesus did it then and He can do it now- through you!

I have been given authority over the devil; I can rebuke him verbally.

Remember that what we truly believe will manifest in our behavior.

Believe that a kingdom mindset has been given to you in Christ. According to 2Tim.1:7, you have been given soundness of mind, a spirit of love and of power, and not of fear. You have been given clarity of thought and sound judgment, wisdom and common sense, the ability to discern and to be disciplined. What an inheritance. We can see truth from God's perspective just as Joseph did. There is no situation that cannot be redeemed by God's perspective. Let's remind each other of that!

The power of God's love is so much greater than the fear or confusion we can feel when going through trials or unfair situations. However, His law of love ruling the Kingdom is greater than any "feeling" you may encounter in this world. The kingdom of God is within you! Turn away from destructive thoughts and feelings and turn to your source of all love, peace, joy, longsuffering/patience, kindness, goodness, faithfulness, gentleness, and self-control. His love never fails! And that Love lives in you!

"But the fruit of the spirit is love, joy, peace, longsuffering, kindness, goodness, faithfulness, gentleness, self-control. Against such there is no law" (Gal.5:22-24 NKJ).

We all need to remember that the Word of God is the riches of heaven, the mysteries of the kingdom revealed to us, and life and health to our body.

Satan hates Kingdom builders, particularly the daughters of the King.

The Bible declares that the serpent and the woman will be enemies until the end (Gen. 3:15 TLB).

Married or single you have an enemy!
Your family is not your enemy.
Your spouse is not your enemy!

With the divorce rate for Christian marriages escalating you can agree that we don't live like marriage has an enemy. We ignore the signs. Satan is understood in the Bible as an active threat, but how many couples live like it? How many couples recognize what Satan is doing in their lives and actually pray against it on a daily basis, together?

You have an enemy and he has been defeated!

"Be self-controlled and alert. Your enemy the devil prowls around like a roaring lion looking for someone to devour. Resist him, standing firm in the faith, because you know that your brothers throughout the world are undergoing the same kind of sufferings" (1 Peter 5:8-9 NIV).

Peter unequivocally informs us that we all are under attack from a real spiritual enemy. Peter describes him as a hungry roaring lion that is waiting for a chance to devour us. It might help us to think about this enemy more as a terrorist or a sniper, cunning, dangerous, and obsessed - looking to destroy everything he can in your life, with no regard for rules of fair play. He hates you. He hates God. He hates the family. And he hates all loving godly relationships.

In unhealthy relationships we need to face our brokenness, confront our style of relating, and realize that the feelings of accusation coming from each other are not really ours.
They are coming from the "accuser of the brethren."

Jesus said "Get thee back Satan!"

"Then I heard a loud voice in heaven say: "Now had come the salvation and the power and the kingdom of our God, and the authority of His Christ. For the accuser of our brothers, who accuses them before our God day and night, has been hurled down". Revelation 12:10 (NIV)

If you don't understand this, you will not understand what is happening in your life or what is happening in your marriage.

If this truth is not what you use to filter daily thoughts, emotions and events,
you will be mislead, deceived, and in the dark!

Light and darkness are the two realties.
Don't live in the grey zone!

Wisdom says:

- Practice finding your source of Life in God, not in others
- Deal with YOUR brokenness and subconscious beliefs
- Learn how to shut down the spiritual attacks that come against your life and your marriage.

Whether you are married or single, you will be amazed at the freedom, love, and joy that will continually flow in your life as you act upon these truths.

You will be free from filtering and processing events, emotions, and thoughts through Satan's deception and outright lies.
And you will be free from doubting one another's hearts.

Sisterhood: Love and Unity:

A daughter of the King is strengthened and reinforced in her new identity when she is connected in fellowship to other sisters-in-Christ.

Sisters-together-in-Christ (STIC) is powerful in love and unity, and in zeal for purity and purpose. As sisters-together-in-Christ they share and reinforce identity as daughters of the King. I once told my sisters-together-in-Christ that we have much in common because "we're all ribs!" Yes, we were fashioned from the rib of a man by the Hand of a Creator God. We did not evolve from a monkey or develop from an explosion in the universe. We were fashioned as the answer to man's problem of aloneness; man needed someone comparable to himself, created in God's image.

Man needs woman, and so does the rest of this world.

The Church needs this marvelous sisterhood and the Lord has called us to communicate His Word of salvation, deliverance, healing, and restoration even to the ends of the earth.

I believe we are the instruments of revival and restoration in these Last Days. He is uniting us in the Spirit of His love and truth. What a powerful destiny!

What does Sisterhood (STIC) look like?

- Fellowship: talking, laughing, smiling, crying, embracing, praying, singing, and sometimes dancing: always learning and growing in friendship with Christ and with one another.
- Growth: sharing knowledge of the Word of God through discussion, study, revelation, meditation, praise and worship, and spiritual gifts.
- Intercession: praying for each other believing for household salvation, deliverance, healing, and restoration.
- Servanthood: serving one another in hostessing and helping one another as personal needs arise.
- Outreach: Invitations to special events, crossing ethnic barriers through gracious hospitality, fund-raising breakfasts and luncheons.

Spiritual Disciplines strengthen and reinforce your new identity and characterize a Beautiful Woman:

1. Praise and Worship

The power of praise and worship cannot be overemphasized. The battle is the Lord's and the victory is ours. When we praise Him for Who He is and for what He has done, spiritual forces are put into motion as the angelic hosts war against the opposing forces. We give thanks and praise for God's will to be accomplished. We enter His gates with thanksgiving for who HE is and what He has done. We sing and dance with the Spirit, just as Miriam led the women in song and in dance after they crossed over the Jordan River on dry ground!

Praise and worship is a powerful weapon against the enemies of doubt and fear, discouragement and confusion. Keep believing and confessing His strength in you and for you, and you *will* see mountains move with the faith of the Lord Jesus Christ. (Psalm 151NKJ).

Praise and worship Him in the sanctuary and praise and worship Him in the bathroom! Praise Him all day and all night long. Be reminded to take your eyes off "self" and your circumstances, and focus your attention completely toward Him and all that He has done for you. He's got His eye on you!

Let's focus on the solution rather than talk about the problem!

2. The Power of Intercession

Interceding for others is a gift of love to them and a blessing for you. Allow the Holy Spirit to pray through you. He helps you confess your own inabilities and fleshy desires, bringing forgiveness and cleansing to your soul each time you pray.

God flows through a "clean" pure in heart vessel, one that is not clogged with carnal "stuff". Together we can agree in prayer according to God's will, and He performs His will here on earth "as it is in heaven".

Believe His Word.
Pray His Word.
Be His Word to others!

3. Prayer with Fasting

Right now I am on a three day Daniel Fast: fruits, vegetables, and whole grains. Lots of water is essential. Not only does this provide a physical rest for my body but also it gives my mind and emotions a rest from distractions and from being in my kitchen preparing food. My focus becomes clearer and my spirit is more responsive to hear from the Lord. Try it. I know you'll like it!

There are many ways to fast from the controlling desires of our flesh. And Isaiah reminds us that it is not only abstinence but also action that is necessary to fulfill God's will in fasting. Looking after the widows and the orphans and your own relatives is a command with a promise.

"Then your light will shine out from the darkness, and the darkness around you shall be as bright as day (Is 58:10 TLB).

Prayer with fasting leads to repentance and action. Praise the Lord!

These simple but powerful disciplines of obedience help to strengthen and reinforce our identity, vision, and purpose. A beautiful beloved daughter of the King is a warrior princess who builds the Kingdom of God within herself and extends the Kingdom of God to others! She conquers new territory for the King. She is always busy doing the Father's business. Remember where you have come from and where you are now seated -at the right Hand of God in Christ, ruling and reigning over all the works of the evil one, prospering in spirit, soul, and body. You are being restored to the very image of God, the image you were created to represent on this earth.

He is alive and He lives in you, and in me, and together with God we are unstoppable!

Chapter 10

Radiant Health: Strong in Spirit, Soul, and Body

"Beloved, I wish above all things that thou mayest prosper and be in health, even as thy soul prospereth" (3 John: 2 KJV).

Truth Application

If you want to understand the condition of your physical state why not look at the state of your soul!

God has designed us to prosper in spirit, soul, and body. He promises us "wholeness"- translated from the Hebrew word "shalom", which includes the meaning of "nothing missing, nothing broken." Every part of us is to experience redemption and newness. We are not only recycled but revitalized!

He wants to beautify us with radiant health that glows from the inside out.

A woman becomes more beautiful as she lives from the inside out. You not only *behold* His radiance and beauty, but also *reflect* His radiance and beauty. Notice that I did not say that we are to reflect perfection. Leave that for the Hollywood air brush.

Radiant health is progressive, and primarily *begins in* our soul. You are beautiful from the inside out! The "beautiful" is in seed form on the inside and will blossom and bear fruit on the outside.

Let's look more closely at the beginning of those above quoted words in 3John:2. Did you notice the "above all else"? Prosperity is a top priority for our God. When we are prosperous and healthy in soul *and body* we become more beautiful inside and out, and we are more able to fulfill the will of God for our lives, in spite of our circumstances, hardships, "insults" or "persecutions". Paul writes to us of these things in 2 Corinthians 13.

We prosper in our spirit, soul, and body as truth reigns in our minds and love rules in our hearts.

We become beautifully radiant.

We are at peace with God, at peace with ourselves, and at peace with others.

Are you beginning to notice that biblical prosperity differs from that of worldly prosperity? The women of the world are becoming more physically attractive on the outside because of all their emphasis on physical beauty, but are they becoming more beautiful on the inside? Isn't it easier to "fix up" the outward rather than work on the inward? For me in my "old" life, it was proven to be easier to change my hair color and to focus on shaping up my body, or buying a new outfit, rather than pursuing a gentle and quiet spirit within.

We live in a world of action and first impressions based on appearances and it is common practice for most women to follow those defining lines. However, beauty defined by the One who created us, is produced on the inside *first.*

Note: While at university I changed my hair color to platinum blonde and then back to brunette again because I was attracting the wrong type of male. I had no idea how to change myself from the inside out at that time in my life, so I kept changing my hair color, which became a *way of life* for me.

The fruit of the Spirit produces such sweetness and depth. This inside beauty shines through to the outside. I strongly believe that enhancing inside beauty with your *own personal style* on the outside is what demonstrates the uniqueness in which you were created. You are not a cookie cutter woman; you are not a cookie cutter Christian. You are one of a kind! Amazing.

Truth Application

You will discover your own personal style as you are set free from conforming to this world's standards.

The glamour of Hollywood and the Runway pales in comparison to the new you! The world is waiting to see something different, something genuine, something true and lasting. The world is waiting for YOU! You reflect His beauty in human form. You are in Christ and He is alive in you! As you enjoy your Lord and your life in Him you become radiant with a new confidence and appreciation for everything.

Beautified with His love and compassion you become like a fresh breeze or a stunning sunset to those who encounter you. He is the One Who beautifies you with His love and compassion. You do not have to strive to be loved by Him or strain to be beautiful!

Let's remember how Psalm 1 enlarges our understanding of how prosperity of soul, is linked to beauty. Read and reread Psalm 1 aloud. That is a true picture of your soul life. You are flourishing in prosperity and beauty.

In **Psalm 1:3** a prosperous soul (your mind, will, and emotions) is compared to a tree planted along a riverbank. The tree bears luscious fruit in each season without fail. Its leaves shall not wither, but flourish (prosper) in all ways. Isn't that fabulous? You have beautiful leaves and lush fruit. Who doesn't want a beautiful mind and the fruit of love, joy, peace, patience, kindness, goodness, faithfulness, gentleness, and self-control?

In **Psalm 1** the metaphor of the tree is compared to the person whose soul is healthy. She has good mental and emotional health as she soaks up a continuous flow of God's love to water and nourish the roots (your spirit), causing the leaves to grow. Planted by the water's edge of His Word, she, the tree, will produce fruit in each season without fail. Being planted refers to the soul who delights in doing everything God wants her to because she meditates on God's laws (precepts, promises, commandments), day and night - continuously thinking about ways to follow Him more closely. Yes it takes some time and lots of practice to learn how to meditate. I still need to ask for the Lord's help to meditate at night. Maybe I should ask for His help not to be tired in the evening!

Soaking in a daily dose of God's love in spirit and in truth causes her to be deeply rooted in that love and truth, just as the tree planted by the water's edge soaks up the water. The tree does not have to struggle to grow. The tree simply soaks up all the good nutrients it needs to blossom and to produce luscious fruit.

Psalm 23 lets us know that a prosperous soul is one that has all its emotional and psychological needs met in Christ. When the Lord is your "Shepherd" you will lack nothing that is needed. He provides *all* that you need *all* the time. You are born and nurtured in abundance not lack, and you will see everything that is good and right within yourself and in your life. You will speak over others' lives with the rich harvest of abundance in them.

Vs. 2,3 Jesus provides the green pastures and still waters of healing and wholeness. You have His peace, His rest, and new strength. Yes, He even gives you the grace to do what honors Him the most as you walk in His righteousness and in His ways.

A prosperous soul is content.

Sheep are completely dependent upon the Shepherd for provision, guidance and protection. When we allow the Lord to guide us we have contentment. Our Good Shepherd knows which green pastures and quiet waters will restore us. We will experience these places only as we obediently follow Him. Going against the Shepherd's leading is actually rebelling against our own best interests for the future. We must remember this the next time we are tempted to go our own way rather than the Shepherd's way.

Remember it is not God who is tempting you to do wrong. Satan is the initiator of temptation to go against God's ways and commandments, so use the authority that Christ has delegated to you to rebuke and bind him. You are free to follow God! Amen!

A prosperous soul is not isolated.

Sheep do not live alone. It is so important not to forget the "assembling together of the believers. God's Word and His presence become magnified as we share our lives together and experience our collective identity as God's sons and daughters, the body of Christ.

A prosperous soul is also refined
in worship and in fellowship.

Beholding Him in worship and fellowship releases our burdens and fills our hearts with gratitude and renewed faith. We are energized. Trusted friendships with our sisters-in-Christ also change our countenance and our lives. Each of us has a measure of faith and love and gifting to pour into one another. We continually receive and give more of His loving grace and mercy. The light of His countenance is upon us. What radiant health.

When the rest of that scripture (3 John 1:2) promises that *"everything you do shall prosper"*, it does not mean immunity from failure or difficulties. Nor is it a guarantee of worldly wealth and earthly happiness. What scripture means by prosperity is this: when God's wisdom is applied to our lives, the fruit it bears in us will be good (Galatians 5) and we will receive God's approval. Loved *and* approved of by God. What more can we ask? As a tree soaks up water and bears luscious fruit, we soak up God's Word, producing attitudes and actions that honor God.

How can you fail to bear fruit when the good seed of God's Word is planted in the good soil of your believing heart?

True prosperity is found in knowing the true value of God's Word.[1] You become productive and blessed in all your ways. As you realize the value of God and His Word you value yourself in increasing measure. His love becomes magnified to you, for you, and in you! What radiant health!

Application

The Book of Psalms lends itself directly to the application of planting the Word of God into the good soil of believing hearts. As you read the Psalms you can release your inhibitions and your imagination. We meet Someone in the Psalms who lets us know through the Psalmists of our deepest hurts, longings, thoughts, and prayers.

Every woman needs someone to talk to who understands her.

The Psalmists depict our intense range of emotion which needs to be heard and understood without judgment. Honest conversation helps to *inform* and *transform* us. God meets us in the Psalms with His unconditional love and understanding. We are totally known by Him and that helps us get to really know ourselves. We eventually recognize an image of ourselves that demonstrates His likeness. Amazing! The Psalms gently push us toward being what God designed us to be - *beautiful women who are loving and living for Him!*

For very many years I clung onto the words of 3 John: 2 and I searched the Psalms for answers to my deepest needs. I had so much illness and distress most of the time. Going to the doctor or to the hospital seemed to be regular occurrences for me. My husband visited the Emergency wing of the hospital many times!

Without believing and clinging onto the truth of those scriptures I know that I would be a very sickly and weak woman today. The Scriptures, particularly the Psalms, let me know that the Lord God knows me inside and out, and that He will use my sometimes feeble faith to cause the fulfillment of His Word in my life. He told me through His Word that *"I will restore health unto you, and I will heal you of your wounds saith the Lord" (Jer. 30:17). "I will restore to you the years the locusts have eaten" (Joel 2:24-26).*

I could fill this page and more by quoting the scriptures God spoke to my heart during those years of emotional instability and physical pain. It is remarkable to me that during such a time, I became convinced I belonged to Him and that He had assumed full responsibility for my life. Yes He really does heal the broken-hearted and set the captives free! Release your life to Him completely

- everything in it to Him. . .every thought, deed, attitude, emotion, and every person and situation.

*His love for me became a reality because
I believed His written Word and said a
simple prayer.
I didn't know I was a sinner needing salvation.*

Prior to being born-again (39 years ago!!!), I knew nothing of the gospel other than Jesus was born, died, and rose again. I never had any idea that Jesus was really alive and that He wanted to live His life in me. I was totally clued out! After reading and paraphrasing selected scripture passages as assigned homework from a Women's group, I started believing what I was reading! The Women's group of Christians I was part of was simply a Morning Out for Moms program at a Mennonite Church. I was a new Mom of a 6 week old baby girl and I desperately needed the outing. I faithfully did the homework from the Mom's group, reading and paraphrasing selected scripture. As a former high school teacher of English Literature I found the assignment easy to do. The discussion group was studying a book entitled <u>Break Free</u>. Little did I know at the time that I was bound up in sin and a captive of the deceptions of the devil, and that it was I who needed to break free.

One day reflecting in my family room, I sensed a Presence in the room. I suddenly realized that it was the Presence of Jesus.

He is alive and real and He seems to be in my family room! I was overwhelmed at this awareness and told Him that I would follow Him anywhere. Weeks later I was in my dining room polishing my dining room table when I sensed His Presence again. This time I began to weep deep within me as I knew, for the very first time, that He had died for **me!!** He loved me enough to be punished, and suffer and die for me! He loves me! I wept for quite a while and as I recall, I didn't finish polishing the dining room table. I knew that He died for me. I had no real understanding of what that meant or what the gospel was all about. I only knew that I had encountered the Presence and Truth of the Living God. That was the result of doing my scripture homework!!!

Power Point

When God's Word is believed and accepted as the simple but ultimate truth, being planted into the good soil of an honest and sincere heart, it bears good fruit, and a harvest of righteousness, with added souls to the Kingdom (see Psalm 126).

I did not know at the time that this Scripture would be fulfilled in my life.

Absolutely incredible!

As you turn to the Psalms in your personal devotional times with the Lord, you will be able to pour out your heart and identify with the psalmists. You will realize you are not alone and you are not "going crazy," nor do you have to believe that what you are going through will never end! You will recognize yourself in the mirror of the psalmists' written words and find comfort, hope, and healing.

As you read **Psalm 1** meditatively, *insert your name for the tree* planted by the living water. Following Jesus wholeheartedly guarantees that we will never lack anything we need. He is always faithful to us, even unto death!

Did you know that Jesus is the least loved and most forgotten of anyone?

Sweet daughter, your love brings Him comfort and joy.
You have captured His heart!

Soul Food: Where Do I Start?

It is imperative to get to know our Savior and Lord through the content of the Gospels. Mathew, Mark, Luke and John, and the book of Acts give us an accurate picture of our God in Christ. You will be surprised to discover what the "real you" is like as well! God in Christ will come alive *to* you and *in* you.

We are able to truly love someone when we know Him as He really is.

Take time to read the gospels as your personal study and devotional time.

It is the truth of the gospel and the revelation by the spirit that transforms us from the inside out. Awesome!

Reading and meditating on Proverbs is just like eating an apple a day to give you good mental and emotional health. It is so easy to follow a proverb each day according to the date. May 1 means that I read Proverbs 1. You will see your soul prosper as you act upon the gained knowledge and understanding of God's ways.

A Simple Guide to Follow

- Ask the Holy Spirit to teach you the truth of the Word of God
- Read the selected passage in The Psalms, Proverbs, or the Gospels.
- Summarize what the **passage** says literally. Paraphrase.
- Ask the Lord what He is saying to you!
- In prayer, commit to obey by His grace, what has been revealed to you,

How Can We Meditate Day and Night?

The more we know of the whole scope of God's Word, the more resources we will have for daily wise decisions that produce good mental and emotional health. Our mind will be filled with the knowledge of the truth of God's Word, appropriating and absorbing the mind of Christ, giving us good strong mental health. Dr. Robert Schuller of California's Crystal Cathedral has said that the best mental health therapy is faith in God and in His Word. We cannot have any greater mental health than a mind filled with faith! A doubtful mind is a like a wave tossed to and fro upon the ocean, producing anxiety, worry, and fear (James 1:6, NKJ).

Good Mental Health in Turn Produces Healthy Emotions.

Thoughts will always be the initiator to our reactions, perceptions and attitudes. The Bible clearly states that *"as a man thinks (in his heart) so is he"* (NKJ).We become what we think, and our subconscious does not differentiate between good or bad thoughts. It is simply a receptacle for whatever we feed it.

Whatever is in the subconscious mind will manifest in our behavior.
We will reap in action what we sow in thought.

170

Our healthy thoughts will produce healthy emotions. We won't be deceived by the lies of the devil when we know the truth and believe the truth. Unhealthy or toxic thoughts based on lies produce very toxic emotions. Both Dr. Don Colbert and Dr. Caroline Leaf explain this in detail. Caroline Leaf's book Who Switched Off My Brain[2] and Dr. Don Colbert's book Deadly Emotions[3] are tremendous resources to convince and instruct you in the power you have to change and renew your mind. They can be found online as well.

The Gospel Applies to Every Part of Our Anatomy and Psychological Make-up.

We are *designed to* think like God. 2 Timothy 1:7NIV states that God has given us a sound mind and a spirit of love and of power for calmness, discipline, and self-control. Believing God's Word changes your thoughts to be aligned with the character and ways of God! Then you know how to act.His truth will set you free. You will be transformed when you give time to know your Creator God and Savior. That old blueprint and wrong image will have no more behavioral power over you.

You will see your reflection in His.

Amazing!

The Holy Spirit is faithful to meet you in your sincere heart's desire to get to know your God and Savior. Here is a "successful" guide for a Devotional Time. So many women tell me that they do not know where to begin or how to spend time with God. Below is a simple but powerful guide which will make that time meaningful and life-changing for you. Remember that we are all learning how to love and to live in His Kingdom!

ACTS Devotional Time

- Adoration
- Confession
- Thanksgiving
- Supplication

Adoration

A mind that is focused on giving thanks for the boundless self-sacrificial love of our Creator in Christ is a very healthy mind. **Psalm 139 and Palm 103** are so wonderful to read in preparation for your thanksgiving, praise, and worship. As you listen to His Word you can agree with Him that what He says is true. He will make it a heart belief as you keep meditating on the truth. When you think about the truth of the gospel (Matthew, Mark, Luke, John, and the Book of Acts) you will know that you are loved beyond measure, and faith is released through that love. It's true. He loves *you* and came to rescue *you,* and Jesus Christ by His Spirit lives in *you*. Yes YOU!

He created you out of love for love, with faith and hope. He never intended you to live in sin, sickness, and shame. As you focus on the truth (not a feeling), you will not mentally live in the past with regret or shame. You can rejoice in the ever new loving- kindness of the Savior each day. As you sit at His feet in adoration He fills your mind and your mouth with good things to think about and to share with others. More of the revelation of Himself is imparted to you each time you spend time together. Your mind is fixed on believing His love, receiving His love and sharing that love.

Read **Psalm 100** to remember that you are His. You belong to Him! It makes adoration so easy when you begin with a Psalm of thanksgiving and praise.

Confession

This is always soul cleansing. Jesus has given you a blood bath for your entire body and you only need to wash your feet. As a new creation in Christ you have been made righteous and approved and accepted by God. You are now the righteousness of God in Christ because of His shed blood. Washing only the dirt (wrong or sinful thoughts, attitudes, feelings, actions) from your feet daily keeps you acting and thinking like the righteousness of God in Christ. You are the daughter of the King! Your confession and His forgiveness brings true repentance. God already knows your weaknesses, failures, doubts, and struggles. So why carry them? Emotions can reveal any unhealed wounds so be sensitive to your emotional state as part of your confession. *A feeling denied is* intensified, so acknowledge all emotions.

Without acknowledgement, destructive emotions will exert control over you on a subliminal level.

Confess them all and be free of any control they are exerting or attempting to exert in your life. For example, until you let go of uncontrolled anger, you will continue to hurt. Anger is a secondary emotion which will cover hurt, disappointment, frustration, fear, helplessness, and other harmful emotions and beliefs. *Anger often is the expression of unmet needs.* Confess your faults, your intentional or unintentional sins, and He is faithful to forgive you and cleanse you of *all* unrighteousness (1John 1:5). Without a daily confession time you will feel unclean and perhaps guilty. And we know that the devil will bring condemnation and judgment at that time.

Is anyone sinning against *you*? Confess and send away the hurt feelings that cause you to view yourself less than you are in Christ. Confess any judgmental attitude toward the offender. A beautiful woman hurts and feels all the emotional pains of others' sinning against her, but she does not hold onto those feelings. They have no power over a daughter of the King any longer. We forgive the sin against us, and do not retain it against ourselves. In this way you will be quick to stay free of the wrong image of yourself. You are a daughter of the King who may have sinned, but you are not a sinner by nature any longer. Praise the powerful Name and sacrifice of Jesus!

Note: A decision to forget the offence/sin breaks the power of any *latent* unforgiveness. You may need to do this many times because Satan will bring the offence back to your remembrance. Continue to remind yourself and the devil that you have been forgiven and believe God's Word that He will use all things together for your good and His glory according to His purposes.

> *"And we know that all things work together for good to those who love God, to those who are called according to His purpose"* (conformed to the image of His Son) (Rom.8:28,29aNKJ).

Then your emotions can heal. Jesus has given you everything you will ever need to live free, to love Him, to love yourself, and to love others-just the way He loves!

- He took your sinfulness and gave you His righteousness
- He took your weakness and gave you His strength.
- He took your sickness and gave you divine health.
- He took every defeat and gave you His victory in its place!

You are the heir of the greatest Exchange ever made.

He said to her, "Daughter, your faith has healed you. Go in peace and be freed from your suffering" (Mark 5:34 NIV).

Thanksgiving

"Enter His gates with thanksgiving and His courts with praise" (Ps. 100:4 ELB).

Thank Him for creating you in His image. He has made a masterpiece (Psalm 139) of divine design. Thank Him for Jesus and all that Christ purchased for you on the cross and by His stripes. Thank Him that all your needs are met in Christ and that He is the Lover of your soul. You have personal blessings He has provided that you can recite before Him. Remember to thank Him! **Psalm 136** is great as a reminder.

Supplication

Make your requests known to the Lord with thanksgiving. Pray for yourself and others from the position *of* victory, not *for* victory. Christ has done it all in paying the debt for your sin and sickness, the curse, the devil and death itself. Pray in His victory!

Pray according to the Word of God that declares you are blessed, deeply loved, highly favored, wise, and in good health.

Your devotional life will become a joy and a delight after you decide to make it a discipline. Your emotional make-up will be anchored in submission to the truth, and not in yielding to whim or fantasy.

Remember:
Your devotional life is based upon dependence, discipline, and obedience, not on feelings or moods.

You will be grounded in His love and Truth.

The more we bask in the radiance of God's presence through thanksgiving (**Psalm 100**), worship in spirit and in the truth, the more we cultivate the spirit of joy within us! Our will becomes surrendered to God's will and there is a serenity and contentment about our "lot" in life.

In other words, if you want the radiant health of a prosperous soul, you can decide to cultivate a heart longing for the presence of God, and for the Word of God. Simply ask Him for it!

Yes, ask God for a heart that *longs* after Him. It's not a natural inclination or desire. Just read the first part of **Psalm 119** for motivation. It seems that we all long for everything else but God.

177

In our natural sinful state we long for what our flesh desires. As Christians we can find it easier to naturally follow our own selfish desires *because* we do not have a heart that longs for and yearns after God. He seems to be the last one on our list, yet we say He is Lord.

"God please forgive us and
help us to put You first."

In the Book of Ezekiel (36:26; 46:23 NKJ) God said He would give us a new heart. We need to believe it. Then our desire and longing for God will become a reality; your heart beating as His. You will never be the same again.

Being loved by Him experientially is the greatest
source of love anyone can possess.
That love makes you emotionally fulfilled and
satisfied.

"My beloved is mine and I am his" (Song of Solomon 2:16 NIV).

"He restores my soul" (Ps.23:3 NKJ).

We get a fuller experience of being loved and made in His image as we see ourselves together as His body- valuable and vital living members from all over this world.

Remember in Genesis God said, "Let *us* make man (humankind) in *our* image." I will give you an analogy to illustrate this. Have you ever gone out on a date with a man who had no body just a head? Sound ridiculous? Well, when you think about Jesus as your Head (because He is the Head of the Church) how can you know and love all of Him if you ignore His body? He is the Head and the rest of Him comes in the form of you and me and all of our other brothers and sisters in Christ. We are His body. Each part is necessary and designed by Him. Don't you need arms to hug you and hands to help you? Yes! His image is also collective not only singular!

We also get the true bigger picture of His love as we have relationships of loving and trusting friendships with other members of His body. Being part of the greater works of the last days means that we function as one body with one Lord! All of us, being born again by the Spirit of God are *first spiritual beings representing His likeness and purpose in human bodies.* Remember that God is Spirit and truth and so the complete and accurate image is seen in spirit and in truth, not by the five senses or personal preferences. We are to know and love one another "after the spirit", meaning that we connect by the spirit when we live in truth and in love.

Paul tells us often to stop being carnal by knowing each other "after the flesh."

We cannot be known by one another for who we really are in Christ, by the flesh.

It's hard
to imagine how big He really is.

The flesh in this context refers to our natural senses and preferences. Neither can we know God by our flesh. He is Spirit and Truth and those who worship Him must do so in spirit and in truth. God is Spirit and Truth without any shadow of darkness in Him!

In order for our love relationship with God to produce good mental and emotional health we must not separate Him from His body. Can you imagine having a relationship with someone who has no body, only a head? Enjoy the friendships of authentic and beautiful Christian women who have made a choice to radiate His love and purposes. Think of joining or beginning a Sisters-Together-In-Christ small group! Even though you may have your own women's group in your local church, an interdenominational group of sisters-together-in-Christ (STIC) will fulfill God's purpose for these end times "... *that [we all] may be one*" (John 17:22 ELB).

A Healthy Prosperous Body

Let's turn our attention *to the connection and effect of our soul to our body.* Paul encourages us to rely upon the indwelling Christ to give us the grace to become all that God has designed us to be, and to do. But we must *first believe* that to be the truth! Then as you practice the disciplines required for a strong healthy soul and body, you will find that His grace really is sufficient to become radiantly beautiful inside and out. God's peace will prevail as you incorporate godly principles for your soul and body. If you neglect either part, you will undoubtedly experience mental, emotional, and/or physical instability. Continued neglect will eventually cause ill health. A little guidance and encouragement presented below will be of tremendous help. Following the necessary disciplines for emotional and physical health will prove well worth the time and effort. You are worth it. Praise God that there are very practical applications for each.

Effective Disciplines for Emotional and Physical Wholeness

1. Think Well

- Your mind can focus on all that is good and right in God, in life, within self and within others. Make a list if you need to be reminded!

- Believing the best and trusting the truth of God's Word releases faith which provides us with the best mental therapy. Faith works through love.
- Journaling is a gift you give yourself. It is a tool in response to emotions as they surface; it clarifies beliefs and hidden thoughts, and facilitates the healing process.

2. Eat Well: Proper Nutrition

- Foods affect your emotional and mental health, particularly your "mood." Clean foods are necessary for proper digestion and elimination. I strongly recommend the *Maximized Living Approach* which encourages changing from eating man made fats to eating God fats; from processed meat to free range and grass fed meat and poultry; from high cholesterol eggs to free run eggs; from white flour and refined sugar to whole grains, almond or coconut flour and raw natural sugar.
- Look for whole or clean foods in their natural state (mostly fruits and vegetables) and buy organic spices (all natural taco seasoning is great). These simple changes have produced better health in every area. It did take me quite a bit of time to find the health food stores and to learn new recipes, so start with one or 2 changes at the start.

Listed below are some of the simplest and most delicious recipes I enjoy preparing and eating:

Breakfast Favorite

10 Grain Pancakes with Cottage Cheese and Berries. (Yum!)

Wash and slice strawberries & set aside

Measure 1 cup 2% cottage cheese per serving

Warm the Organic pure Maple Syrup

Prepare pancakes from 10 grain mix (I use Bob's Red Mill 10 Grain Pancake and Waffle Mix)and cook in skillet

Place 2 or more pancakes on a warmed plate. Add cottage cheese then top with strawberries. Add the warmed maple syrup. YUM!

Lunch Favorite

Field Greens Salad plus Protein

(Spinach Salad, Pear & Pecan Salad, Caesar Salad, Greek Salad, Creativity Salad)

Basic Salad: Start with prepared organic spinach/ field greens/romaine lettuce or arugula, depending on your above selected salad.

Basic Dressing: This is the God fat way to dress your salads!

Extra virgin Olive Oil,

Freshly squeezed lemon, or lime

Sea salt to taste

Add: Herbs & spices for Spinach Salad

Organic pure Maple Syrup for Pear and Nut Salad

freshly grated garlic for Caesar Salad

Balsamic vinegar for Greek Salad.

Use your imagination and creativity by adding avocado, or dried fruit or Grain Dijon Mustard to any of the above salads.

Add protein: Choose from hard boiled eggs/ chicken/ beef/ fish/ nuts & seeds/tofu/Feta, Goat cheese, Swiss, and Parmesan, etc. Enjoy it all as a main or side dish.

Optional: whole grain tortilla wrap.

Fresh or organic ingredients make all the difference.
You will love the difference!

Supper Favorite

Turkey or Chicken Burgers with Sautéed Mushroom and Onions

In a large pan add butter and olive oil (desired amount) to stir fry onions and mushrooms. Let onions and mushrooms simmer while you cook the turkey/chicken burgers in another skillet.

1 lb. free range ground turkey or chicken

½ cup finely chopped celery

¼ cup chopped red onion

1 Tbsp. fresh or dried Tarragon leaves

1 Tbsp. Dijon mustard

½ tsp. all purpose seasoning, organic or Spike Seasoning, or ½ tsp. sea salt

¼ tsp. pepper

2 eggs (free run)

3 Tbsp olive oil, cold pressed (use coconut oil for a fabulous flavor)

Preheat frying pan and oil on low heat. In mixing bowl combine ground poultry with celery, onion, tarragon, and mustard. Add seasoning, pepper, and eggs. Shape into patties. Place on frying pan and increase to medium low heat. Fry for approx. 7 mins. per side until browned. Serve immediately.

Delicious High Energy Snacks

Apple slices with raw almond butter or raw peanut butter

Hummus with bell peppers, carrot sticks, celery

Guacamole with bell peppers

Handful of almonds, or pumpkin seeds and dried or fresh fruit

Dr. Don Colbert in his book Stress Less[4] informs us that a change in your diet will actually change the level of stress in your life. What we feed our bodies has a direct effect on our souls just as our soul's condition directly affects our bodies. For encouragement and reinforcement on creating emotional and mental health, and physical wellness, I recommend the following:

The 7 Pillars of Health *by Dr. Don Colbert*

Body by God *by Ben Learner.*

Maximized Living Seminars

3. Exercise Well

- Muscle building stimulates hormones that help with fat loss. Therefore modify the exercises that build and sustain muscle no matter what your physical condition; keep building and maintaining muscle mass. If you are a "people person" join a gym or health club. If you like a little music as well, try out Curves. Known to reduce stress and body fat is the building up of muscle.

- Walking alone, with a friend, or with your iPod is relaxing and clears your thinking. It is also slimming for the hips!

    Don't let the word discipline throw you because discipline simply involves structured training. *Learning to plan and schedule what your body needs* will create discipline and self control. I heard Joyce Meyer say that all we need to do, to develop the fruit of self control, is exercise it. I need the help of the Holy Spirit to keep me working on that!

4. Sleep Well

- Seven to eight hours in a cool quiet darkened room without distractions helps. Six hours of sleep may suit you better. Let your body inform you. People who have suffered insomnia were able to sleep when they were instructed to wear socks to bed (go figure that one out). Warm milk before bed is supposed to work as well. Don't forget the winding down time (a warm sudsy shower or bubble bath?), and develop a habit of going to bed an hour earlier than usual *so you can get up early to enjoy your devotional time.* (always need to keep working on that one!) Regular hours of uninterrupted sleep also create glowing skin. Always sleep on a clean pillowcase, preferably satin. These are just a few beauty tips for beneficial sleep. Curl up in His arms and let Him look after all your concerns and cares.

"For so He gives His beloved sleep" (Psalm 127:2 NKJ).

"He neither sleeps nor slumbers "(Psalm 121:4 ELB).

5. Forgive Often

- Forgive everyone all of the time. The sooner the better for you! The Bible tells us not to go to bed angry, so talk things out with the Lord or whomever, and forgive when necessary, whether you feel like it or not. Forgiving is not easy because of the injustice; and the people who need forgiveness usually do not deserve it. That's what makes forgiveness *an act of mercy and grace.* I certainly didn't deserve to be forgiven by Christ when I was doing my own thing sinning and trespassing against the God of Love. But He forgave me while I was still sinning against Him! And *He* was betrayed by one of His very own beloved disciples! Christ uttered words of forgiveness when He was suffering, and died a cruel underserved death on a Roman cross for you and for me, to save us from all that sinning and from our very own human sinful nature! Forgive others as Christ as forgiven you. Amen.

"And Jesus prayed, Father, forgive them, for they know not what they do" (Luke 23:34 ELB).

- God is the vindicator! We can trust Him to take care of the injustice and the other person(s) involved. Diligently seek Him for His perspective and His healing. He is your rewarder for such obedience to His ways. His love will not fail you even though others will fail you. . . and more than once!

- Unforgiveness is like a deadly disease. I remember someone stating that unforgiveness is like taking poison and expecting the other person to die. So often we feel we have a right to be angry because of the injustice. Righteous indignation must be taken to the cross. The power of all harmful things to hurt you or destroy you has been broken through Christ. Don't hang on to the pain and an unforgiving self-righteous attitude that says His victory is not enough.

6. Be at Peace with God, Self and Others

- A must read is 1Peter 5:7-10.

  Did you know that it is a source of pride to hang onto your concerns? Do you think you can handle any of them better than the Lord? I didn't realize that hidden pride wants to prevent me from trusting the Lord with everything that concerns or hurts me. Disappointments, discouragements, delays, and losses are all part of those things that we can carry within us. God cares about them all and wants to carry them away. He gives grace to the humble (James 4:6b NKJ).

- Be at peace with yourself.

Your relationship to yourself is the one that can build you up or tear you down!

Learn to accept, to love, and to cherish yourself just the way God does. Base your opinion of yourself upon the truth of what God says. This is not a selfish desire or pursuit!! Remember that you love and care for others as you love and care for yourself. This is the greatest commandment next to loving God with all your heart, strength, and mind.

". . .You shall love your neighbor as yourself."
(Matt.22:37 NKJ; Mk 12:30-31 NKJ).

Do you know that the most important and influential opinion of yourself is made by you?

- Be at peace with others

    When you think well about others, giving them the benefit of the doubt, you will be at peace. The Bible teaches us not to judge others otherwise we will be judged. Nobody owes you your pound of flesh because the Lord sends rain on the good and on the bad alike. Be like God and pray a blessing on everyone you know. Most people suffer from a lack of God's love and forgiveness. Everyone needs love and forgiveness. Pray for that without ceasing!

Also consider the benefit of following these practical principles for sound emotional and mental health:

1. Do what's right in spite of your feelings (forego the good feeling)

    Remember: Don't base reality on your feelings. Feelings are not facts or truth. . .they are emotions that can change in an instant. If I fail at something I may *feel* like a failure, but that does not make it the truth about who I am.

The devil gains a stronghold in this area if he can convince us that our feelings are reality and we become defeated by believing his lies and accusations. Don't allow the wrong voice to control your feelings and determine your attitude. Know the truth as God sees it. This is sound and stable emotional and mental health!

2. Sacrifice now for future investment (Holy Spirit enabled)

3. Make a positive affirmation of self-in-Christ.

Believe in your heart and confess with your mouth the truth of who you are in Christ. Verbally reinforce and share your new biblical identity with your Sisters-Together-In-Christ (STIC). Why do this? So the lies of the devil will have no place in your mind or emotions. The human mind doesn't discern or care what we think about. Whatever we think will sow a seed and later reap a harvest.

You will become what you think about so plant your new identity and new vision in your mind.

- Believe that you will succeed and you will. *"With God all things are possible" (Matt.19:26 NIV).*

- Focus on your assets and abilities. Get feedback from others.
- Have faith in those God-given abilities and gifts.

4. Erect Boundaries

As you learn to highly value and esteem yourself in Christ, which allows you to esteem others even better than yourself, you will need to set up boundaries to grow strong in purpose and focus. For example, *personal boundaries will help you "draw the line" over what you will and will not do, think, look at, or speak about.* Going after everything you see or desire is all vanity and a chasing after the wind without any profit (Solomon 2:10, 11NKJ). *Begin to develop wisdom goals* in all areas of personal, social, work or ministry, relationships, and finances.

Two books I recommend by Dr. Henry Cloud and Dr. John Townsend are: **Boundaries** and **Boundaries *in* Marriage.**

Do not allow anyone to use or abuse you. And that includes YOU! Personal boundaries will promote beautiful radiant health.

5. Pajama Day

God rested on the seventh day of Creation and said all that He has created is good. Have a Pajama Day one out of seven days to rest your mind, emotions, and body, and say to yourself that everything in your life is working for your good and for God's glory, according to His purposes for you. Get yourself a comfortable and pretty pair of pajamas and enjoy the refreshing of being the new you without guilt or regret. If you don't want to wear pajamas that's perfectly okay. All you need is the mindset! I am not the same beautiful woman without a Pajama Day once a week. Amen!

Discussion and Application

1. A beautiful woman is known by her character. What kind of fruit are you producing? Are you a picture of good mental and emotional health?
2. Refer to Psalm 1. Describe yourself as a tree. Where are you planted? In what condition are your leaves?
3. Read and reread Psalm 23 aloud and sense the connection to Psalm 1. Does Psalm 23 make any promises for the different stages and circumstances of your life?
4. Review the guideline for good emotional and mental health. Which discipline needs your attention today? Why?

Conclusion

As you develop a strong spirit and a healthy soul you will find it easier to have and maintain a healthy body. It will surprise you to see just how much beauty is released into your life through both.

We can be adorned with *Radiant* health no matter what age or stage of life. I was in my late fifties when I discovered Maximized Living Seminars and over 50 when I went back to school to study for a Masters Degree at Seminary. In Australia at the Hillsong Women's Conference in 2005 I learned for the first time that "woman" was created as the answer not the problem! Now at 66 years of age, I am in my best emotional, mental, and physical health (Some have said that I look like I'm in my forties!)

God is so amazing. He never gives up on us, and always believes the best of us. We are His deeply beloved, highly favored, and greatly blessed daughters who are "risen, empowered, and beautiful to the core."

"They looked to Him and were radiant
And their faces were not ashamed" Psalm
34:5 (NKJ)

Chapter 11

Collective Identity: The Beautiful Bride of Christ

The Daughters of the King are an indispensable and vital part of the Beautiful Bride of Christ. You are greatly desired, needed, and equipped as the Beautiful Bride of Christ. You are married to the King of Kings! Even now the Lord has asked you to consider Him *"your Husband"/ "Ishi" (Hosea 2:16 NKJ)*. What a thrill to be the Bride chosen to reign with her Bridegroom forever!

As the church and body of Christ we are the *collective identity of the Beautiful Woman;* sisters and brothers in Christ who live by faith in the Spirit and in Truth. We are spiritual beings who have a soul and live on this earth in a physical body. Yes, we function in a physical body; however, the "body" of Christ is a spiritual body. Christ in His resurrected form has no physical properties. He is completely alive in a spiritual body that will never die. We are part of His spiritual "body" because we are born of His Spirit.

No flesh can inherit the Kingdom of God because *"the Kingdom of God is not eating and drinking but righteousness, peace, and joy in the Holy Spirit" (Rom.14;17 NKJ).* We live in a new spiritual Kingdom under the rule of the King of all kings!

The Bride, as the body of Christ, is the *collective image of God!* She is beautiful because she is a reflection and representation of the image of God Who is Three in One living in harmony and in order. *She is God's beautiful woman!* There is no striving or competition in the Godhead. There is no striving or competition in the spirit of the individual believer or collective Bride. We have been given a new nature with everything we need for harmony and order creating unity in the Spirit.

Foundational Truths Regarding the Beautiful Bride of Christ

1. The Resurrected Christ is the Bridegroom and He is the Head of the body of Christ, His Beautiful Bride.
2. The Bride has many different parts in her spiritual body and is to function according to divine design in order for it to be fully alive, just like a physical body.
3. The Spiritual Realm is the *highest realm of authority* to rule each individual part and to rule over the collective body.
4. All spiritual authority to rule over the forces of darkness has been delegated by Christ to God's sons and daughters.

What Does This Have to Do with Our Restored Femininity in the Image of God?

Well, our beauty is cultivated in the spirit by the Spirit and by the revelation and application of the truth of God's Word. Our spirit affects our female psychological soul which influences our physical state. As daughters of the King and sisters in the body of Christ we are enabled to cultivate the fruit of the Spirit, displaying the very *nature* of God with a distinctive feminine heart. We are created to be feminine in our radiant beauty and expression. We have the opportunity to openly express our bridal love for the Bridegroom individually and collectively. Remember how Mary Magdeline worshipped at the feet of Jesus, wiping His feet with her tears? Nowhere does it record a man doing this. If you study the passage you will notice that Jesus says that wherever the gospel is preached so must this act of worship by Mary be recalled.

Do we understand that we are betrothed to Jesus, our soon and coming Bridegroom? The picture of a Bride is so full of femininity, poise, and grace!

Jesus created our beautiful sexuality and honors us in it.
Our feminine heart is restored!

Discussion and Application

1. Are we excited about our collective identity as the Bride of Christ? Describe the collective image of God.
2. Is our affection and devotion given to Christ above all else, or are we "cheating" on Him with other competing loves?
3. Are we spending time in preparation for His return?
4. Does our conversation include Him when we gather together or does the focus of our attention remain on us?
5. Do we dress and adorn ourselves to please Him or do we dress and adorn ourselves to attract the attention and/or approval of others?
6. What is the highest realm of authority and who possesses it? Do you need to make some changes in your thinking as well as your attire?

These are some of the questions I believe we need to ask ourselves and each other more than once. We need to change the way we think –to have our minds renewed by the truth of God's Word. We need to purify our hearts with His forgiveness and grace, *releasing all that does not belong to us in our new position as the risen, empowered, and beautiful to the core daughter of the King! This is true repentance.*

*Repentance produces the joy-filled life.
This makes us truly beautiful!*

I was first introduced to the idea of repentance by a great and lovely elderly woman of God named Mother Basilea Schlink. Being exposed to her writings and personality (on Video) when I was a new Christian, helped me ponder my need to have joy and inner beauty. It never occurred to me that I needed to have a mind change and on-going forgiveness for that to happen. Her story and writings intrigued me. I wasn't hearing any messages about repentance anywhere else. Church leadership and Women's groups seemed to be telling me to try harder to be more Christ-like and to do more. I felt somewhat defeated in both of those areas even though I continued to give and to serve.

Even as a new Christian I sensed that what Mother Basilea Schlink was saying was true. God's <u>grace</u> of repentance (changing my mind to agree with God's Word) produces the newness of God's Life for my actions and gives me the joy of the Lord. Those truths I heard from Mother Basilea Schlink were deposited on the inside of me and were effective later in my life to help set me free from personal conflicts pertaining to obsessive performance affirmation and perfectionism.

*She was a "spiritual mother of the faith" for me in
my early years*

Application

Do you need to change how you think to agree with how God thinks? In which area(s) does your mind need to conform to the truth of God's Word?

A renewed or changed mind is the fuel for the Holy Spirit engine to work. When we have "cheated "on our Lord or been neglectful or prideful, we can repent. We can confess and decide to change our ways to line up with the truth of the Word of God. His forgiveness and love for us is real. At these times of struggle and confusion we need to be reassured of God's love for us. We will not fall into Satan's trap of condemnation or yield to the deception and lies he injects into our thoughts. We remain fixed in our new identity and position as co-heir with Jesus.

God's unconditional love toward us is described in 1 Corinthian 13. Take a moment now to remind yourself of what it says by rereading it several times.This is how God loves us continually, and that love is *in* us, and *for* us, and is to be expressed *through* us to others. Let's read it with a realization that He loves us beyond any human love, all of the time and forever!

Reflection: Do we look like His Bride?

Are you living like a woman who is loved?

Are you clothed with the humility of His forgiveness and grace?

Can you say that "I am my Beloved's and He is mine?" And that "I have no other "gods' before Him?"

Godliness with contentment makes you beautiful. Godliness becomes you and is pleasing to the Lord, and is also very attractive to this world. So many Christian women have not realized this. *Godliness displays itself in a separated life from worldliness. The things of this world have lost their hold on your heart! Your submission to confident and complete trust in the Lord and His Word has* produced the beauty of holiness and humility, befitting the Beautiful Woman, the Beautiful Bride.

Willingly submitting to God also allows us to willingly submit to the human authorities He has placed over us. This makes us "sweet" and very desirable. I prayed for years to have godliness with contentment. Contentment to me is like eating a good meal. I was content to have a good meal. Then I ate a meal that was gourmet and organic. Not only was I content but completely satisfied. In John 17 Jesus promises us that a relationship with Him is not only one of contentment but one that truly satisfies! *Contentment with godliness and deep satisfaction is most rewarding and fulfilling for the beautiful woman and the beautiful Bride.*

Your mandate is to be the transforming agent on this earth!

The Bride of Christ is empowered to do the works of Jesus!

This beautiful godly woman is definitely not a wimp. She is characterized as a *princess warrior* in the Kingdom, equipped with delegated authority from Christ in the spiritual realm. That authority in the spiritual realm will effect change in the natural realm. *God's Kingdom rules in His Bride.* His righteousness, His truth, and His agape love are released to a hurting and confused world through her. She has been given the faith, the grace, and the favor to accomplish His will on earth as it is in heaven. Amen!

We are to decree and declare that His kingdom come and His will be done on this earth as it is in heaven-
<u>*first and foremost in us!*</u>

God rules through His body from the heavens to direct the affairs on earth. We as the Church, the Beautiful Bride, are the government of God at home and in the world. His kingdom in and through us rules *by agape love in all we declare and do.* We can understand that our collective mandate from God to rule (have dominion) parallels that of our individual mandate.

The On-Going Battle

The on-going battle of good versus evil is not a battle against flesh and blood but against powers and principalities and spiritual rulers in high places (Eph.6:12 NKJ). We always battle from a position of victory. Christ has won the battle against Satan, and all evil. This is part of the armor for princess warriors.

Our *position in battle* is one of worship. Our hearts are filled with thanksgiving and praise to our beloved Bridegroom. When trouble comes, by grace, we sing and dance and praise the King of all kings and Conqueror over all evil declaring His Word to be fulfilled and His will to be done, as it is in heaven. *Circumstances do not dictate our response to our King and Bridegroom.* We are free to declare His wonderful victory.

- *Declare to the enemy the Words of the Lord despite the negative reports. We live by faith and not by sight.*
- *Talk back to the devil and He will retreat! Satan does not obey our thoughts, only our authoritative words!*
- *Bless those who curse you; pray for those who mistreat you.*

Decide to overcome being shy or self conscious. The Holy Spirit will stir up the gift in you and will speak through you: *It will take much practice before you do this automatically and with ease. So begin now!*

The battle belongs to the Lord and the victory is ours. The Beautiful Bride must feed and nourish her spirit more than her mind and emotions for this spiritual battle.. We all must avoid a busy mind, confusion, and frustration like the plague. (How's that for an old expression?) The language and music of worship and praise will fill our soul and fuel our spirit. With renewed minds corporate praise and worship makes the Bride come alive in beauty and in power!

Yes, this way of living in the Kingdom beautifies us with a crown of loving-kindness and good deeds. Negative thoughts and emotions cannot exert control over you as you worship in spirit and in truth. We, as His daughters and sons, declare, like our King, those things that are not in existence as though they already exist, according to God's Word, in the Name and authority of Jesus Christ. We believe God to fulfill His Word.

This has proven itself over and over as according to God's Word, I declared salvation for my husband and children when I was a new Christian. Then I declared that each would be baptized in water and in the Holy Spirit, speaking in a new heavenly language. Yes, all my children and husband are born of the Spirit, water baptized and all speak in a heavenly language (tongues). I will be writing a book on Household Salvation in the future.

Life in the Kingdom is lived in the spirit by faith and not by sight. Faith always works through Love.

Truth:
The church of Jesus Christ is built upon revelation knowledge of the truth, and faith in Jesus as the Son of the Living God (Matt.16:17-19).
The Church is not built upon Peter!
The church of Jesus Christ is not a denomination or religion.

We as the church, The Beautiful Bride, are a spiritual household of faith and have a spiritual heritage that supersedes all denominations and religious cultures. Jesus is the Head of His church and we are His body. His body is defined and functions in spirit and in truth as He is Spirit and Truth.

"God is Spirit, and those who worship Him must worship in spirit and truth" (Jn.4:24 NKJ).

In no way are we to create a god of our own imagination. We have the truth of who He is and who we are in the written Word of God. Paul teaches us that we as God's children, His body, are to be recognized and known "after the spirit", being baptized with the

Holy Spirit and fire (Matt.3:11 NKJ).We are not called to know one another by the works of our flesh. There is neither male nor female in the spirit so we must love in the power of God's gracious agape love, as brothers and sisters in Christ. There is purity in God's agape and Phileo love. We can greet each other with a "holy kiss" or a warm embrace with this kind of love, void of sensuality. Remember that sensuality belongs in the marriage bedroom!

The body of Christ is spirit not flesh.
We are created to function according to God's
divine design not man's traditions.

Our functional representation is not only to reveal the character of the living and true God, but also to build up and extend His Kingdom, having dominion over the earth. God gave Adam and Eve dominion over the whole earth, not each other! We will be restored in that function as we appropriate our delegated authority over all that is against the character and will of Almighty God.

First and foremost, as mentioned earlier, we as the "risen, empowered, and beautiful to the core", daughters of the King need to repent of our own disobedience in not behaving or thinking in the character and will of God. *Remember that repentance is turning away from our own thinking to adopt and agree with God's thoughts and ways.* His grace is sufficient for ". . .where sin abounds, grace abounded more" (Rom.5:20 NKJ). We need to ask the Holy Spirit to make us aware of the need to confess and repent of any thought, emotion, attitude or action that is ungodly. These thoughts and emotions just "pop" up at times. Sometimes we will need to verbally rebuke the devil when he harasses or bombards us with an unrelenting ungodly thought, emotion, or attitude.

When we wholeheartedly desire to walk in His character and ways He gives us the grace to do so. Humility will clothe us and love and forgiveness will keep us strong.

God is the Initiator of Oneness

God has created us as teleological beings, always wanting to move toward something; so He is our Helper in moving us toward oneness in the Spirit (Jn.17: 11; 21-23 NKJ). . . "that they may be one", Jesus said. He wants us to move in the direction of unity in the spirit *not* unity in denomination or religion. As His daughters we will beautify the Bride in our unity. As we love one another and know one another after the spirit, there will be no competition or strife among us. We are true friends.

We cannot operate in our Kingdom authority when we are in competition, strife, or unforgiveness.

How many women do you know that compete and strive against one another? The daughters of the King have been set free from such ill will. We are overcomers in Christ of all competition, comparison, strife, envy and jealousy.

We must remember that *our functional representation is for us to have dominion over the earth, individually and collectively.* We can't do that if we are divided against each other.

Be transformed from a victim to a victor; from a worrier to a warrior; from a thermometer to a thermostat, setting the climate in our environment, rather than allowing the environment of worldliness and evil to be the influencer.

God releases His grace to us through the power of the Holy Spirit when we repent. We all need to give up control and to submit to God's Word. We all need to submit and yield to the leading of His Spirit Who guides and instructs us in the ways of righteousness. We yield to the King and His kingdom of righteousness, agape love, peace, and joy in the Holy Spirit. We become more beautiful and more desirable as we repent. His goodness has led us there (2Peter3:9 NIV).

We also need to be willing to be made new through the necessary suffering that allows us to experience the power of His resurrection and the fellowship of His sufferings (Phil.3:9-11 NKJ). I see this "suffering" similar to pregnancy and labor. We are carried through uncomfortable and sometimes difficult stages of pregnancy, and then the labor pains begin. Labor pains are painful but we know new life is on the way. The end result is new birth! Don't think it strange when you experience trials, temptations, and sufferings. New life is on the way!

1Peter and Isaiah 48:10 teach us that suffering according to God's will is always redemptive!

We are purified and protected forever (Ps. 12:: 6-7 ELB).

Jesus is coming back for a bride *"without spot or wrinkle" (Eph.5:26-28 NKJ)*. His shed blood is more than enough spot remover to clean every stain of sin and He can iron out all the wrinkles. Faith in the power of the shed blood of Christ in forgiveness, deliverance, and healing removes all the wrinkles and spots. *Don't try to clean your own bridal gown!* Just believe and receive His forgiveness, healing and deliverance because of His sacrificial love for you, and your gown will become spotless.

In Ephesians 4 Paul calls us to live in love, being kind to one another, tenderhearted, forgiving one another, even as God in Christ forgave you. When we decide to forgive others, God's grace enables us to do so, and allows for our own healing. This is a process that takes time, just like the healing of a physical wound. Deepening our fellowship with the Lord will enable us to release emotional pain and unforgiveness. We will need to go through a grieving process before we can heal.

Grief is the flood of feelings we experience over any great loss. Society brings numbness to this process in different ways, all of which are designed to "numb the pain" rather than release the pain. Many people are afraid to show deep emotion, so we as the daughters of the King, can draw close to others in love and comfort in their grieving. The one grieving needs to be loved and listened to with sensitivity. Grieving people get tired and exhausted so they need proper nutrition and rest. How we handle loss now is an indication of how we will handle loss later in life. Take the time to reflect upon what you really believe about yourself, about God and about others during the grieving process.

Forgiveness also needs to be understood as a process once the decision is made. It is like a dance that you learn step by step toward complete freedom in joy and gratitude. Without true grieving there is no true heart forgiveness and healing. Jesus taught us to forgive from the heart which means that we must examine our heart and allow the Holy Spirit and others to help us to recover and to be free.

Many members of the Body of Christ still need to experience this process of grieving and healing. Let us be agents of healing to one another so that we will have a message of hope and healing to our hurting world.

We can do this.
His grace is sufficient!

Paul writes to the Philippians to **"stand fast in one spirit, with one mind, striving together for the faith of the gospel"** *(Phil.12:7b NIV).*

". . .God resists the proud but gives grace to the humble" *(1Pet. 5:5; Jas.4:6 NIV).*

In Ephesians 5 Paul stresses that we are to be "imitators of God" (Eph.5: 1 NIV). **"for you were once in darkness, but now you are light in the Lord. Walk as children of light (for the fruit of the spirit is in all goodness, righteousness, and truth), finding out what is acceptable to the Lord and have no fellowship with the unfruitful works of darkness, but rather expose them"** *(Eph.5:.8-11ELB).*

"Awake you who sleep,
Arise from the dead,
And Christ will give you light" (Eph. 5:14).

Visions Regarding the Bride

The first vision appeared to me in Toronto. I was at the Spirit-Led Prayer Conference in September of 2011. Remember how the

Lord had led me there by His intimate knowledge of me and my circumstances? Well, I did take time by myself to worship in song and dance, (and much repentance) in my hotel room. Yes, I love to dance. I began ballet lessons at the age of four.I was so pleased that the room was equipped with an IPod stereo player. God knows everything I need!!

The picture that entered my mind during this worship time alone with God was that of a Bride reclining on her side in a sleeping position. She was wearing a long white gown of pure silk, and seemed motionless. I watched as she opened her eyes, and then began to stretch a little as she extended her body from head to toe.

The Sleeping Bride was being awakened.

*****

While in New Zealand attending a Women's' Conference in March 2012, I had another encounter of seeing the Bride. This time the Beautiful Bride who looked exactly the same in her reclining position, was not only awakened, but was rising upward, but not by her own strength. Two white doves were lifting her gown at both ends as she was effortlessly moved upward. It was amazing to behold. This Beautiful Bride is rising up in faith by the power of the Holy Spirit and not by human effort.

"Not by might, not by power, but by My Spirit, says the Lord". Zech. 4:6.

This effortless movement of the Bride encourages us that God is able to work His perfect will in and through us by His grace and Spirit. There is no struggle or strife - just being carried upward by faith that works through love toward the high calling of Christ Jesus our Lord. Wonderful!

In September 2013 I was surprised when I saw another vision of The Bride. This time she was in an upright position, holding each end of her gown in hand and twirling round and round. She was looking up as she twirled and I could see her radiant smile lovingly gazing toward Jesus her King. She was delightful and joyful. It looked like she was having "fun"! Did I say fun? I remember my husband telling me that the word "fun" was not in his family's vocabulary. That was over 40 years ago.

As I watched the Bride elegantly twirling, I distinctly heard the Spirit of God,, say that He wants to release "play" in His body through the dance. Yes, joy filled play and fun **by dancing unto the Lord.** Now remember that His body is spirit living in a physical shell. At this exact time, seeing the Bride twirl in sheer delight, I was in an indoor swimming pool all alone singing and dancing unto the Lord. I was having so much fun! As I sang and danced in the buoyant lift of the water with child-like faith, I sensed a surge and lift of the Holy Spirit.

Later that week I needed to inquire of the Lord for further meaning and interpretation. The vision and my singing and dancing in the pool were related. Loving God can be fun! I was dancing in the spirit with my Lord and King and that rejoicing in Him, with my physical body, was like a child at play. It became a supernatural "high."

There is a fun, safe, and healthy way to "get high"!

Biblically this is sound and true. Moses' (and Aaron's) sister Miriam, the prophetess danced before the Lord in rejoicing for the Lord's deliverance (Exodus 15:19-21 NKJ). "King David *danced* before the Lord with all his might; and David *was* wearing a linen ephod" (2 Samuel 6:13-15NKJ).

> **"Let them praise His name with the dance;**
> **Let them sing praises to Him with the timbrel and harp"**
> **(PS. 149:3 NKJ).**

Psalm 149 and Psalm 150 are filled with instructions to praise our God with instruments, with singing, and with dancing. Try it; you may be pleasantly surprised! God definitely enjoys His people, and even He rejoices over us with singing (Zeph. 3:17 NKJV).To me it seems that we not only have eternal life, but we also have eternal youth by *our childlike faith and rejoicing.*

I see the reality of these visions in my own life, and I know that God's plans for His universal Bride will be fulfilled!

Beautiful Bride, the King desires to dance with you!

The Bride has been awoken and is being empowered by the Holy Spirit. In humility and adoration she worships. In returning to her first love and in rejoicing in her Bridegroom and soon and coming King, she is radiantly beautiful and most powerful.

Is that a picture of you beautiful woman?

The Daughters of the King in Relationship to the Sons of the King

We as the Bride of Christ are not strangers or casual acquaintances but brothers and sisters in Christ who need to learn how to regard one another as new creations, born of the Spirit. Men don't need to dominate women to get their strength and women don't need to dominate men to get their strength. They complete and complement each other in their functional representation.

Being created male and female in the image of God

is not a blueprint for competition,
but one of completion and representation.

Together we portray the collective
identity of the image of God.

Strong men and strong women do not fight each other; they know how to fight the fight of faith against the real enemy Satan. Satan hates this and uses all forms of deception to divide men and women. In general men are influenced by what they see, and Satan knows this as well, so he will use enticing spirits, seduction, and flattery to influence them. This leads them astray from the truth and sometimes from home. Women, in general are influenced by what they feel. So Satan takes advantage of these women who will confuse real love with lust or physical attraction. As women, we either have our power in sexual purity or we exercise our feminine power in sexual perversion, which easily distracts and seduces men.

How will you use your feminine power?

Just a note about sensuality as opposed to sexual perversion is that God designed sensuality between husband and wife as part of their sexual intimacy. It is therefore sanctioned by God to be sensuous in the bedroom with your spouse. It is not sanctioned by God to dress or behave sensually beyond those parameters! Low cleavage and tight fitting clothes are easy targets for enticing and seducing spirits. You don't want to have any part in that! Amen?

- Know the role God has designed for you, then dress for it.
- Declare it in the way you behave toward the men in the body of Christ and in the world.
- Don't send mixed messages!
- The way you present yourself is directly a result of your relationship with God.

We as His daughters exert influence by:

- Being godly not worldly
- Being faithful, not famous;
- Trusting in God not in man;
- Fearing the Lord not fearing man.

And He says you are powerful in beauty and holiness!

We as the daughters of the King and Bride of Christ, represent a global church with a distinctive world view. We are one in the Spirit as we love God "with all our heart and with all our soul and strength and love our neighbor as ourselves". This is the first and greatest commandment given by God. For all the law is fulfilled in doing this

(*Gal.5:14NKJ*). We are beautified by His love to love ourselves and to love others.

Remember that your intimate relationship with God gives you a <u>healthy thriving relationship with yourself in unconditional love</u>.

Only then are you able to love others unconditionally.

Now What?

In these Last Days characterized by signs and wonders, earthquakes, natural disasters, cold hearts, unbelief, licentiousness, immorality, persecution, world government, fulfilled prophesies, and the eventual mark of the beast, how does the Lord want us to live? How do we as beautiful women, His beautiful daughters and Bride, conduct ourselves in our daily life before He returns?

Jesus tells us more than once to "fear not." He knows the destructive force of fear, worry and anxiety; He repeats the warning in scripture many times and in different ways. While studying The Book of Revelation as a student in Seminary I was given a jolt when I first was asked the question of *what or who do I fear more* than God. Often we are asked who or what we *love* more than God. The

Book of Revelation draws our attention to whom or what we *fear* more than God.

Pause and prayerfully think for a moment. Is there anyone or anything you fear more than God? We cannot live as women in love if we entertain fear. We are to fear God and God only (Deut.6 NKJ).The good news is that God's perfect love for us and in us will give us the love and reverence for Him that will cast out all our fears (1Jn.4:18 NIV). We don't need to be fearful or anxious about tomorrow in these Last Days.

As Beautiful Women and daughters of the King, I believe we must share common pursuits. Here are four principles to live by based on the Scriptures.

1. Lordship Romans 12: 1, 2

Lordship involves taking your hands off your own life because you belong to God. Make the decision and commitment to Jesus Christ as your CEO and Lord. Become a disciple and a living sacrifice. Stay close to godly women, your sisters-in-Christ, who model this.

2. Membership Romans12: 4, 5

The church is not an organization, but a living organism with Jesus as the Head. We belong to one another because we belong to Him. We must see our need for each other's part of the body, otherwise we will foster pride and arrogance among us. Together as the His beautiful daughters and the Beautiful Bride, we build and extend His Kingdom.

3. Stewardship Romans 12:6-8

Discover and use your spiritual gifts. Spiritual gifts are given to everyone. Local church home groups and small groups such as STIC give opportunity to recognize and nurture our spiritual gifts.

4. Fellowship Romans 12: 9-13

I searched the meaning of fellowship in its Greek translation because it seems that the term can be misunderstood. *The biblical word "fellowship" in the Greek is "koinonia" and describes the beautiful relationship of faith which connects true Christians to God and to all other true believers.* Koinonia does not refer to worldly socializing. The Word of God states that we are to have "fellowship" (koinonia) with the Lord and fellowship with each other in much the same way. Sisters-together-in Christ in faith and in love builds up His kingdom within each of us and in the sisterhood, strengthening our part of the body of Christ. This is true fellowship.

It's very insightful to look up meanings of the Greek translations and root definitions. Try it!

Loving each other without hypocrisy and prefer-ring one anoth.er fosters a spirit of love.

Scripture Informs Us of Jesus' Priorities in these Last Days

Luke 12:25-41 tells us:

- Do not be caught off guard; stay alert in spiritual realities
- Keep your lamps burning full of the Holy Spirit. You are the Light in this present darkness and are protected by the armor of faith and love
- Focus on eternal treasures
- Exercise wisdom in waiting for His return with vigilance, justice, and faithfulness
- Stay awake even though you have been waiting a long time. Watch for His return and stay sober
- Be faithful in discharging your duties; to whom much is given much is required. Jesus rewards faithfulness. He gives both earthly rewards and heavenly eternal rewards. God is always faithful to us.

As we keep Matt.6:33 a top priority for our spiritual life, we won't forget such a long list.

You may need to look up Matt.6:33!

1 Thessalonians 5: 11-24 tells us to:

- Encourage each other to build each other up, and offer supportive words or actions
- Give honor and high esteem with wholehearted love to your spiritual leaders
- Avoid quarreling among yourselves
- Warn the lazy
- Comfort the frightened
- Tenderly care for the weak
- Practice patience
- Resist revenge
- Be joyful
- Pray continuously
- Be thankful
- Do not quench the Holy Spirit
- Do not despise those who prophesy
- Keep away from evil
- Rely upon God's constant help

You may want to copy this for reference and encouragement!

Each living part of the body must nourish and receive nourishment from the other parts to sustain life - just like the human body. Scripture confirms that we as the daughters of the King and

His Bride are to be active in nourishing our own spiritual lives and then loving and giving *first* to the household of faith, particularly the *widows,* the *orphans* and *the poor*! These can be right in your own biological family, within your relatives, or those around you. Looking after our own extended family is a command.

Remember that the church is a living organism that needs each part functioning according to divine design in order to sustain the life of the Body.
The church is not an organization or a corporation!

I pray with Paul IThess.5: 23 -24;

"May the God of peace Himself make you entirely pure and devoted to God; and may your spirit and soul and body be kept strong and blameless until that day when our Lord Jesus Christ comes back again. God Who called you to become His child, will do all this for you, just as He promised."

"Who is and was and Who is to come, the Almighty (Rev.2:8)

After you discuss the content of this section it would be most appropriate to share Communion with each other, recalling what the Lord has done on the cross for each of you. When you know yourself as a Beautiful Woman and Bride *because of what Christ has done for you and in you*, you desire to give Him whole-hearted thanks and praise, and true worship. Your heart overflows with gratitude to your Heavenly Father in being His risen, empowered, and beautiful to the core daughter. And you want to receive continuous forgiveness and cleansing keeping your heart pure for Him.

Remember to forgive yourself with the forgiveness given to you by Christ. Do not hold unforgiveness toward yourself or against anyone else, particularly in the Body of Christ. He forgives you upon confession and heals and restores you because of His stripes and atoning death and resurrection (1 Pet.2:24 NIV). Do not hold your sin against yourself. Christ does not hold your sin against you. He forgave you all of it so release all of it at the cross. Wonderful!

Communion

Christ's death reveals to us the amazing grace, the riches of God's mercy, and His *great* love toward us (Eph.2:4-10 NIV). Through His great suffering and atoning death Jesus fulfilled all the redemptive types and prophecies in the Old Testament. He and He alone fulfills all of the Law. Blessed be His Name!

In preparation for Communion, the following Scriptures with commentaries can be read aloud, followed by a time of worship and reflection:

Vines Expository Dictionary of N.T. "Jesus was aggressively and viciously tested, tempted and tried throughout all of His life by Satan, evil men and circumstances, but in spite of all this evil pressure against Him, He lived a perfect sinless life. Jesus was the perfect sacrifice for sin, the sinless Lamb of God. It is not the scourging of Jesus, but the precious atoning blood of Jesus that brings us healing of body, soul, and spirit to us."

He was scourged and punished for us. In Isaiah 53:5 we read, "And with His stripes"; the word used for "stripes," in the Hebrew, is "**chaburah**," Strong 2250. It is in the singular, and it literally means, "a bruise," the result of a blow on the skin. As we have already seen, "stripes," in 1Peter.2v24, is "**molopi**," Strong 3468. It likewise is in the singular, "a bruise," this reveals to us that the body, soul, and spirit of Jesus was one massive and terrible bruise. He voluntarily suffered being beaten black and blue in body, soul, and spirit, for us.

Barnes writes about "chaburah." "It is not a flesh wound; it does not draw blood; but the blood and other humours are collected under the skin." End of quote. The scourging Jesus received, mangled His flesh, and produced many dozens of deep bleeding wounds in His flesh - terrible wounds that even reached and exposed Christ's bones. So we can see that Isaiah 53:5 is speaking of something more than this scourging. The inner bruising that the kind and gentle soul of Jesus suffered during this dreadful beating was even worse than the mangling of His flesh. He was despised and rejected by those He came to save; the inner bruising and pain of this was immense. See Lk.19:41-44.

Jesus bravely endured terrible bruising of His body, soul and spirit, for all of His adult life. An examination of Is.53:5 shows that this bruising is referring to the whole of Christ's life, and not just in His scourging and the events around His atoning death. In Is.53:4, the Hebrew word for the King James Version, **"sorrows," is "mak'ob" Strong 4341,** which can speak both of physical and mental pain. The commentary by the eminent Hebrew scholars **Keil & Delitzsch** on "mak'ob," is very enlightening. It states, **"He was [makᵃ'obwt 4341) 'iysh 376)] a man of sorrow of heart in all its forms, i.e. a man whose chief distinction was that His life was one of constant painful endurance."** End of quote. This comment on "mak'ob" reveals the enormous painful pressures that were inflicted on Jesus during the whole of His adult life.

In Is.53:5, "bruised," is "daka" Strong 1792, which means, "to be broken in pieces, to be utterly shattered and crushed", by calamities and trials. See Job.6:9 and Ps.72:4. It speaks of the most severe inward and outward sufferings. In purchasing our redemption, Jesus was under such a weight of sorrows that He was broken in pieces, utterly shattered and crushed to the earth. Men said that

Jesus suffered because of some great sin of His own, but they were dreadfully and totally wrong; God did not smite Him for His own sins, but for ours.

> ***1Pet.2v24.*** *"Who His own self bare our sins in His own body on the tree that we, being dead to sins, should live unto righteousness: by whose stripes ye were healed." (KJV)*

In **Is.53:4** God's promise of healing is an emphatic "SURELY," and "VERILY," not a doubtful "maybe." Jesus informs us in the account of the healing of the paralyzed man in Mt.9:1-8., Mk.2:1-12, and Lk.5:17-26, *that healing of the body should be an expected attendant and result of healing of the soul and forgiveness.* This is confirmed by Is.53:4, where God deals with healing of the body in an unambiguous and very direct and powerful way.

In **Is.53v4,** "surely, "is "aken," a strong and forceful word, meaning truly, surely, indeed. God reveals the totally emphatic nature of His promise of physical healing. We know that *healing of the soul is more important than healing of the body, but here God puts a "surely" on healing of the body;* it appears that He knew how the Jews and the Church would neglect, and fail to take hold of this "charismata" of Divine grace. The translation by Keil & Delitzsch, gives the true sense of **Is.53:4.** *"VERILY He hath borne our diseases and our pains: He hath laden them upon Himself; but we regarded Him as one stricken, smitten of God, and afflicted."*

After these readings it seems appropriate to pause and reflect on the pain and suffering inflicted upon Jesus. It was beyond anything we will ever have to endure; the innocent suffering and dying for the guilty! Worship Him, the Lamb of God.

Declare all the benefits of His scourging, death, and resurrection that you have inherited as His daughter. Allow yourself to go deep into the heart of God's love and provision for you.

Isaiah 53:4-5

You, Lord have taken my griefs (sicknesses, weaknesses, and distresses) and carried my sorrows and pains. You were wounded for my transgressions, bruised for my guilt and iniquities; the punishment needed for my peace and well-being was upon You, Jesus, and by Your stripes I am healed and made whole.

Forgiveness and healing of the spirit and soul gives us the opportunity to be healed in our physical bodies.

Jesus suffered and died not only to forgive us and to pay the debt for all our sin, but also to release us from the power of that sinful nature, from the power of Satan, sickness, and from the power of death itself. Healing of spirit, soul, and body is part of our salvation. Redemption affects every area of our lives. The symbols of the Bread and the Wine cover everything!

We are partners with God in a New Covenant initiated and kept faithful by God (Isaiah 66:22).

Could He do more?

In the simplest of terms, I will say that Jesus took upon Himself and crucified everything ugly in me and in you, so that you and I could be everything beautiful in Him!
A divine exchange!

Beautiful Woman: the Spirit-filled you.

Beautiful Woman: His Spirit-filled Bride

Restored in the very image of God!

Amazing!

Reflection and Discussion

My question to you, Beautiful Woman, is simply this: where are you right at this moment in your life?

Are you living the abundant Life of faith, hope and love that Jesus died to give you?

The Abundant Life in Christ *is not a competition of who is the most Christ-like.* Do not measure yourself with others in this. Measure yourself by attainable goals of obedience to God's will, and compare yourself to no one but Christ.

Christ-likeness and the portrayal of that beautiful image of God in you as a Beautiful Woman, is the *result* of your willing obedience to those God given goals, and His provision of unlimited amazing grace.

Where do you need to grow spiritually as a Beautiful Woman and Daughter of the King?

1. *In knowledge*: through study and application of the Word of God of who God is, who you are in Christ, and of how God has designed life in His Kingdom
2. *In Receiving and experiencing:* God's forgiveness and grace, His deliverance, healing and wholeness; redemption for an unsurrendered area of your life?
3. *In Releasing and developing:* your gifting and abilities in service to the body of Christ, your sisterhood, or to others?

All 3 components are part of an on-going cyclic process of growth. *You and I both need to be continually growing in our revelation knowledge of the truth and in our kingdom experience. Amen?*

Are you flourishing or stagnating?

A small group of intimate fellowship with your sisters-together-in-Christ (STIC) will foster and nurture your growth in all three areas. True sisterhood and friendship is a gift from our Heavenly Father to each one of His daughters. Together we each derive deeper meaning and significance in our lives, and that impacts our contribution to the rest of the body of Christ, the Beautiful Bride, and to our world.

Sisters-Together-in-Christ is not a Bible Study group, although its foundational truths are all biblically based. The emphasis of being sisters together is just that; a shared life not a lonely life. Women learn interactively and grow through sharing.

A strong sisterhood not only reinforces the local church but also initiates revival, healing and wholeness, *and* restoration of God's divine design for His beautiful daughters. Also, we as the daughters of the King are vitally connected together as sisters in Christ with the rest of the body to portray the ultimate Beautiful Woman- the Bride of Christ.

Sisters need to be together to grow and to strengthen their identity as . . . "risen, empowered, and beautiful to the core"- daughters of the King! Sisters need each other!

I have designed Beautiful Woman as a guide and manual for women's fellowship groups such as STIC.

Won't you consider getting together in a small group?

It only takes a spark to get a fire going!

The world is waiting to see a truly Beautiful Woman and God is waiting to see a truly Beautiful Bride!

Remembering you in His Love,

Your sister-together-in-Christ,

Judith

Contact Information: STIC International

judithlenore@live.com

Endnotes

1   Life Application Bible Commentary, p.817.

2   Leaf, Caroline Who Switched Off My Brain? Thomas Nelson; New edition (Nov 3 2009).

3   Colbert, Dan Deadly Emotions Understand the Mind-Body-Spirit Connection That Can Heal or Destroy You. Thomas Nelson (May 10 2006).

4   Stress Less: Break the power of worry, fear, and other unhealthy habits. Siloam (May 13, 2008.

CPSIA information can be obtained at www.ICGtesting.com
Printed in the USA
BVOW03s0026030614

355196BV00008B/48/P